VOLUME 41

MIKOYAN GUREVICH
MiG-29 FULCRUM

YEFIM GORDON AND PETER DAVISON

specialtypress

PUBLISHERS AND WHOLESALERS

Published by
Specialty Press Publishers and Wholesalers
39966 Grand Avenue
North Branch, MN 55056
United States of America
(800) 895-4585 or (651) 277-1400
http://www.specialtypress.com

Distributed in the UK and Europe by
Midland Publishing
4 Watling Drive
Hinckley LE10 3EY, England
Tel: 01455 254 450 Fax: 01455 233 737
http://www.midlandcountiessuperstore.com

ISBN-13 978-1-58007-085-0
ISBN-10 1-58007-085-X

Printed in China

Cover: *RSK MiG chief pilot Pavel Vlasov demonstrates the agility and sleek lines of the MiG-29M2. The aircraft is a land-based version of the naval MiG-29K. (Yefim Gordon)*

Title page: *MiG-29 05 Red (izdeliye 9-13) on a test flight from the Akhtoobinsk test airfield, showing the wing-mounted bomb racks. These can carry 100 kg or 250 kg bombs. The intake louvers may be opened during low speed flight.*

Back top right: *Mikoyan retained MiG-29 (izdeliye 9.12) numbered 10 Blue for demonstration and training purposes. This probably explains the immaculate paint scheme. (RSK MiG archive)*

Back top left: *The cockpit of the upgraded MiG-29SMT-II features the new navigation suite with ring laser gyros, on board INS, and satellite link. (Yefim Gordon)*

Back bottom: *Unlike the MiG-29UB, the UBT combat trainer has full weapons capability. The prototype, 304 Blue, is seen here at Zhukovskiy. The front cockpit is virtually identical to that of the SMT, and the rear features three large LCDs. It first flew on August 25, 1998 and appeared at Farnborough, England, nine days later.*

TABLE OF CONTENTS

Mikoyan Gurevich MiG-29 Fulcrum

ACKNOWLEDGMENTS

THE AUTHORS WISH TO EXPRESS THEIR SINCERE THANKS TO:

Mikhail R. Val'denberg, former MiG-29 chief project engineer;

Valeriy V. Novikov, current MiG-29 chief project engineer;

Vano A. Mikoyan, deputy MiG-29 chief project engineer;

Lev B. Bol'shakov, a leading ANPK MiG officer;

Sepgey P. Belyasnik, a leading engineer at ANPK MiG;

Valentin S. Vetlitskiy, artist;

Andrey Yurgenson, draftsman;

Andrey V. Fomin at GosNIIAS;

Anatoliy A. Komarov, VPK-MAPO;

Viktor Drooshlyakov, aviation writer and photographer;

Vladimir Petrov at LII;

Mikhail Ye. Yevdokimov, my son, for his computer skills and support;

Dmitriy S. Komissarov – the book could not have been accomplished without his excellent translation.

INTRODUCTION

By the end of the 1960s, most air forces had a well-developed aircraft industry using second-generation jet fighters – the MiG-21 Fishbed, the F-4 Phantom II, the F-5 Freedom Fighter, and the Mirage III. These fighters were high performance (a top speed of Mach 2.0 or better and a 19,000- to 20,000 m/62,335 to 65,616 ft. service ceiling), carried guided air-to-air missile (AAM) armament, and fire-control radar enabling day-and-night, all-weather operations. Simultaneously, third-generation fighters were emerging, such as the MiG-23 Flogger, the Mirage F.1, and the SAAB JA/AJ-37 Viggen in Sweden. No quantum leap in performance was needed at this stage. The main requirements were longer range, better maneuverability and versatility, with the ability to operate from semi-prepared airstrips.

These were to enter service in the early 1970s, along with upgraded versions of the MiG-21 and F-4. By then, however, work had started on fourth-generation aircraft that would form the backbone of NATO and Warsaw Pact air forces in the next decade. The USA announced the FX (Fighter Experimental) program in March 1966. Boeing, Lockheed, North American, and later Republic entered the competition.

Originally, the single-seat twin-engine FX was to have a 27-ton (59,523-lb) gross weight and a top speed of Mach 3. The new general operational requirement (GOR) called for a lightweight fighter armed with only an internal gun and short-range AAMs. Later, the USAF revised the GOR to include fire-control radar and medium-range AAMs. Gross weight was set in the 20-ton (44,091-lb) class with a top speed at Mach 2.5.

US aircraft manufacturers began design work in 1969; McDonnell Douglas won the FX contest with the F-15 Eagle, securing a contract in December. The prototype YF-15A took off on July 27, 1972, and deliveries of production F-15As commenced in November 1974. In the early 1970s it was decided to complement the F-15 with a much lighter and cheaper aircraft grossing at 9 to 10 tons (19,841 to 22,045 lbs). It would have simpler avionics and a limited weapons range (internal gun and short-range AAMs only), but high maneuverability. The LWF (Light Weight Fighter) program was announced in January 1972, with the MiG-21 as a reference point.

In February 1972 General Dynamics, Northrop, Boeing, LTV-

This MiG-17PFU fighter-interceptor is a true 1950s fighter interceptor. The PFU version was armed with four AAMs that had the conventional gun removed. More than 5,000 MiG-17 Frescos were built worldwide. (RSK MiG archive).

A MiG-19PM fighter-interceptor with four RS-2-US AAMs. As in the MiG-17, the guns were replaced by a missile capability. Although retired from the Soviet and Eastern Block Air Forces, many "Farmers" still serve in China and Pakistan. (Yefim Gordon archive)

Aerospace, and Lockheed submitted their proposals for the LWF contest. GD's Model 401 and Northrop's P.600 were selected for full-scale development. In April, GD and Northrop were awarded contracts for the completion and testing of two fighter prototypes as the YF-16 and YF-17, respectively. The YF-16 won in January 1975. The USAF requested that the aircraft be given strike capability under the ACF (Air Combat Fighter) program. The F-16A Fighting Falcon made its first flight on December 8, 1976, and entered production in August 1978.

A MiG-21SM Fishbed frontline fighter with four FAB-100 bombs and two R-3S AAMs on the strip. This family of aircraft, developed in numerous versions, was by far the most widely used combat aircraft in the world in the 1970s. (RSK MiG Archive)

This Polish AF MiG-23MF frontline fighter is seen carrying two R-24R and four R-60M AAMs at Slupsk in northern Poland. Produced in large numbers since 1970, this third-generation interceptor has only recently been withdrawn from regular service. (Waclaw Holys)

WARBIRD**TECH**
SERIES

THE CONCEPT

The FFI/PLMI programs

In the late 1960s the Soviet Union was also working on the fourth-generation fighter concept. The Soviet aerospace industry began considering enhancing combat capabilities with new AAMs and a sophisticated weapons control system. All three of the Soviet Union's leading fighter makers joined the effort. These were Mikoyan, aka OKB-155 or MMZ "Zenit"; Sukhoi, aka MZ "Koolon" (Coulomb); and Yakovlev, aka OKB-115 or MMZ "Skorost" (Speed).

In 1971 the Soviet Ministry of Defence issued the first GOR for a fourth-generation fighter tentatively designated PFI *(perspektivnyy frontovoy istrebeetel'* – advanced tactical fighter). The primary roles included close-in fighter combat with short-range AAMs and an internal gun, and intercepting aerial targets at long range with medium-range AAMs. Other roles included providing top cover and defense of important targets, destroying enemy vehicles, escorting heavy aircraft, performing tactical reconnaissance, and destroying small ground targets in daytime with bombs, unguided rockets, and gunfire.

The aircraft had to possess "look-down/shoot-down" capability and operate in any weather conditions, day and night, in an active and passive electronic countermeasures (ECM) environment. The F-15, Northrop P.530, and YF-17 were regarded as the PFI's principal adversaries. Typical aerial targets in the interceptor or "hunter-killer" role included the F-4E, GD F-111A, Tornado, and Jaguar.

High maneuverability was attained by improving the lift/drag ratio and installing lightweight, powerful, and fuel-efficient engines to achieve a thrust-to-weight ratio higher than one. The integrated weapons control system (WCS) featured digital computers, and an infrared search and track (IRST) unit to complement the customary radar. The armament comprises a fast-firing gun and new short- and medium-range AAMs.

The Mikoyan OKB started work in 1970 on the MiG-29 program under Gleb Ye. Lozino-Lozinskiy, chief project engineer for the MiG-25MP heavy interceptor (the future MiG-31). The actual work on the fighter's general arrangement, however, was directed by preliminary design (PD) section chief A. A. Choomachenko, a prominent

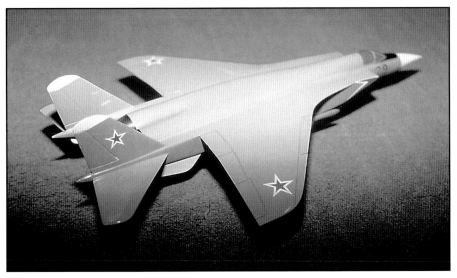

Two views of this model depict the MiG-29 at an early development stage. The aircraft is a mix of the MiG-25 and the future MiG-29. Note the familiar twin fins masking the twin exhausts of the aft-mounted engines. (Yefim Gordon)

aerodynamicist. Two major research bodies were actively involved in the program. The Central Aerodynamics & Hydrodynamics Institute worked on general arrangement, while the State Research Institute of Aircraft Systems (GosNIIAS) worked on the avionics. The engineers considered both conventional arrangements and the so-called integral layout with wings and fuselage blended into a single lifting body.

Much thought was given to the powerplant. Building on operational experience with the best third-generation fighters, Mikoyan opted for a twin-engine aircraft with two lateral intakes. This improved survivability in combat and reduced attrition in peacetime.

An early configuration of the MiG-29 had shoulder-mounted trapezoidal wings, a low-mounted horizontal tail and a single fin and rudder. The wings featured leading-edge root extensions (LERXes) and full-span leading-edge slats. The sharply raked two-dimensional air intakes with horizontal airflow control-ramps were strongly reminiscent of the MiG-25 Foxbat interceptor or the F-15. It featured six underwing hardpoints. Another was a crossbreed of the MiG-29 and the MiG-31 with boxy Foxbat-style air intakes. The nose-gear unit had twin wheels while the main units featured tandem twin-wheel bogies.

A third study used the integral layout with the fuselage, wings, and engine nacelles all blended together. This was a light fighter with a normal gross weight of some 13.5 tons (29,761 lbs). Thus it was not only lighter than other Mikoyan projects, but also lighter than Sukhoi's entry for the PFI competition, which was the T-10 (the future Su-27) with a normal TOW of 21 tons (46,296 lbs). Another advantage of the integral layout of the prominent LERXes was an internal gun location. The aircraft

Here are two views of a MiG-29A display model on General Designer Rostislav A. Belyakov's desk. Belyakov succeeded Artyom Mikoyan, founder of the famous manufacturer. Note how the paperwork very fittingly dominates the plane. (stills from a Mikoyan video).

was shorter than the actual MiG-29 and had a wing area of only 25 m² (268.8 sq. ft).

In 1971 research institutes decided that the Air Force should have several kinds of fighters with weapons systems optimized for the various mission types. An interceptor needed good acceleration and rate of climb, heavy armament, and capable avionics giving it "look-down/shoot-down" capability. An escort fighter needs to have sufficient range to operate 250-300 km (138-166 nm) beyond the

frontlines. High maneuverability, a high thrust-to-weight ratio, a wide speed range, and special short-range missiles were a must for close-in combat. The solution was to build two basic types that complemented each other: An advanced tactical fighter (PFI) and an advanced light fighter (PLMI, later LFI) optimized for operations above friendly territory and the tactical battle area – that is, 100-150 km (55-83 nm) beyond the frontline.

The PFI had a sizeable internal fuel and ordnance load and a com-

prehensive navigation, communications, electronic support measures (ESM) suite, and a specially configured avionics and weapons fit. Conversely, the PLMI was as easy to build and maintain as possible, using semi-prepared airstrips and operated by average-skill pilots and ground personnel. Its armament was limited to two medium-range AAMs and short-range weapons. The PFI and PLMI would account for 30-35% and 65-70% of the fighter force, countering the F-16 and the F-15, respectively.

In 1972 the VVS issued a revised request for proposals. The Mikoyan OKB submitted two versions of the MiG-29 project; Yakovlev entered the Yak-45M light fighter and the Yak-47 heavy fighter, while Sukhoi's entries were the T10-1 and T10-2. After evaluating the projects, the Air Force tasked the Sukhoi and Mikoyan with building the heavy PFI and LFI, respectively; Yakovlev walked away empty-handed.

MiG-29 (izdeliye 9.11) and MiG-29A (izdeliye 9.11A) Light Tactical Fighter (Advanced Development Projects)

In 1973 the fighter force re-equipment research was largely complete, with TsNII-30 issued SORs for the two types with revisions based on research results. The most stringent demands applied to the avionics, primarily the WCS. The fire-control radar was to work in multiple wavebands and be capable of detecting and tracking multiple targets. The aircraft were equipped with an optoelectronic targeting systems comprising an infared search and track (IRST) unit and a laser rangefinder. The cockpit was to feature a head-up display (HUD) and a cathode-ray tube (CRT) indicator.

The intended S-29 radar was substituted by the production "Sapfeer-23ML" (Sapphire) radar, which was fitted to the MiG-23ML Flogger-G. The original MiG-29 version, equipped with the S-29 radar, bore the manufacturer's designation izdeliye 9.11, while the "stopgap" version with MiG-23 avionics and armament was designated 9.11A. Quite simply, "9" stood for [MiG-2]9 while 11 was probably an allusion to some obscure reason for the manufacturer's designation of the "true" Flogger prototypes (izdeliye 23-11). Production costs of the MiG-29 would be little more than half those of the T-10.

Work on the MiG-29A project proceeded, and on July 15, 1974, the General Designer formally approved 1/20-scale drawings of the MiG-29A.

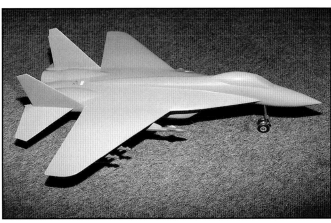

Four views of other MiG-29 and MiG-29A models show the raised cockpit, for good all-round visibility and many features common to fourth-generation fighters of today. (Yefim Gordon)

Originally, Western analysts erroneously believed the MiG-29 to have variable geometry. With the F-111 and Tornado high on Western shopping lists, this was to be expected. (artist's impression from a Western magazine)

The smoothly blended wings and fuselage minimized drag and maximized lift throughout the speed range, while providing ample internal space for fuel and avionics. The wings featured prominent LERXes for better lift at high alpha and powerful high-lift devices (automatic leading-edge flaps, trailing-edge flaps, and flaperons). The stabilators were deflected differentially for roll control, augmenting the ailerons and enabling the aircraft to maneuver vigorously throughout its flight envelope.

The axes of the stabilator hinges were inclined slightly downwards to increase momentum. To maintain a 90° angle between the vertical and horizontal tails, the fins were canted slightly outwards. This made the aircraft statically stable (unlike the T-10, which was statically unstable).

The advantages of the twin-engine layout could be fully utilized by fitting advanced jet engines with low specific fuel consumptions (SFC) and high specific thrusts. Soviet engine designers started working on such engines in the late 1960s. The MiG-29 required an afterburning turbofan in the 7,500-8,500 kgp (16,534-18,738 lb st) thrust class. The Izotov OKB offered such an engine – the RD-33 rated at 8,300 kgp (18,298 lb st). Before long, however, competition showed up in the form of the Tumanskiy OKB with the R67-300 afterburning turbofan rated at 7,500 kgp, and an unofficial contest began.

Tumanskiy regarded his engine's lower dry weight as a strong point; however, Mikoyan engineers were skeptical about this. The point was that the R67-300 was a three-shaft turbofan, while the RD-33 was a two-shaft turbofan. By 1974 the powerplant had been finalized. The RD-33 (a.k.a. *izdeliye* 88) had a specified thrust of 5,040 kgp (11,111 lb st) dry/8,300 kgp (18,298 lb st) reheat and a bypass ratio of 0.475. Using

Izotov's accessory gearbox-drive gave an overall weight saving of about 250 kg (551 lbs).

The in-spaced nacelles and the low-slung intakes made the MiG-29 engines vulnerable to foreign object damage (FOD). On the ground the main air intakes were blanked-off completely by perforated panels (FOD protection doors) hinged at the top. The engines breathed through a series of spring-loaded blow-in doors on the upper sides of the LERXes. During rotation, the FOD protection doors swung up into a horizontal position, triggered by weight off the nose gear, allowing the engines to operate normally. The dorsal blow-in doors closed automatically.

The integrated weapons control system (WCS) developed by NIIAS was one of the most important systems. The MiG-29 is the world's first fighter to have three targeting systems – a pulse-Doppler fire-control

radar with "look-down/shoot-down" capability, an IRST, and a helmet-mounted sight (HMS). The IRST was located in a transparent "ball" offset to starboard, ahead of the windscreen.

After considering a fly-by-wire (FBW) control system, the engineers decided to play it safe and opted for a conventional system with mechanical linkages. This featured irreversible hydraulic actuators in all three circuits, and an artificial-feel unit to facilitate flying and reduce pilot fatigue during prolonged high-G maneuvers.

On June 26, 1974, development of the MiG-29 light tactical fighter was approved. The development program proceeded in two parallel lines. The "pure" version featured advanced mission avionics and weapons, while the downgraded MiG-29A had simplified radar and weapons based on current production models. The idea of a "cheap" light tactical fighter was

actively supported by the MoD, while the MiG-29 with new radar and missiles still had to be accepted.

Both versions had identical airframes, powerplants, and systems. The MiG-29A featured the SUV-23ML-2 (SUV-29A) WCS. It included the Phazotron "Yantar" (Amber) fire-control radar with associated analog computer and target illumination channel for missiles with semi-active radar homing (SARH), the OEPrNK-29A optoelectronic targeting/navigation suite, and data transfer equipment for feeding target data to the missiles' guidance units, etc. The OEPrNK-29A was comprised of the OEPS-29A optoelectronic targeting system, an HUD, a direct-vision CRT display, an "Orbita-20" digital computer, and an SN-29A navigation system. The MiG-29A was armed with an AO-17A twin-barrel 30-mm gun with 150 rounds.

The "proper" MiG-29 differed from the "entry-level" MiG-29A

mainly in having an SUV-29 (S-29) WCS comprising the RLPK-29 and the OEPrNK-29 (S-31) optoelectronic targeting/navigation suite. The latter was almost identical to that of the MiG-29A but featured a helmet-mounted sight. The gun and air-to-ground weapons were identical in both versions, but the missile armament was totally new. In standard configuration, the MiG-29 carried two K-27 medium-range AAMs and four K-14 or K-73 short-range AAMs. Alternatively, six K-14, K-13M1, K-60M, or K-73 missiles could be carried. In the strike/CAS role, the MiG-29A's combat efficiency was two to four times that of the MiG-21PFM Fishbed-F.

On January 19, 1976, the Central Committee of the Communist Party and the Council of Ministers issued a new directive by ordering the development of two fighters – the light MiG-29 and the heavy Su-27. Both types were to pass their

This MiG-29 full-scale mockup in the Mikoyan experimental factory's assembly shop is still supported on floor jacks, possibly for undercarriage demonstrations. (Mikoyan OKB archive)

State acceptance trials in 1977. This was the official go-ahead – at long last. The two aircraft featured advanced WCSs and highly effective new-generation weapons matching or surpassing those of the F-15 and F-16. That took care of the "two versions issue"; the cheap MiG-29A was cancelled, and the OKB concentrated wholly on the MiG-29 as originally proposed.

An R&D program code-named "Soyuz" aided a lot in the development of radars for the new-generation fighters. The main contractor under the Soyuz program was NPO "Istok," which designed and built three prototypes of a fire-control radar also known as "Soyuz." It was a pulse-Doppler radar broadly similar to the Hughes Electronics AN/APG-65 fitted to the F/A-18.

MiG-29E Experimental Fighter Project

The Su-27 and MiG-29 were the first Soviet fighters with digital avionics. The Mikoyan OKB had to undertake a special R&D program named "Feniks" (Phoenix) to tackle the processing problems. Under this, the BTsK-29 digital avionics suite would be developed and tested on the purpose-built MiG-29E experimental fighter.

The BTsK-29 avionics suite and the MiG-29E never got beyond the PD stage. The results of the research effort were later put to good use, however. The institute built a special S-2900 simulation complex jointly with the Mikoyan OKB. Data obtained on the KPM-2300 combat simulator enabled the engineers to estimate how the MiG-29 would fare against the F-15 and F-16 in combat.

MiG-29 (izdeliye 9.12) and MiG-29A (izdeliye 9.12A) Light Tactical Fighter (Definitive Projects)

The MiG-29 project was finally frozen in 1977, even though preparation of drawings and project documents had gone on steadily for four years. When the 1/20-scale drawings of the MiG-29A were approved, General Designer Rostislav A. Belyakov had deemed it necessary to increase wing area from 34 m2 (365.6 sq. ft) to 38 m2 (408.6 sq. ft). The re-winged fighter received a new manufacturer's designation 9.12; the "entry-level" version with MiG-23 avionics and armament became 9.12A.

The integral layout provided a good lift/drag ratio and ample structural strength reserves, enabling the aircraft to pull high G loads and maneuver at high AOAs. Wing lift was increased by means of camber, programmable automatic leading-edge flaps, trailing-edge flaps, and flaperons. The LERXes increased wing lift at high alpha, reducing the risk of stalling and/or spinning. The multi-mode air intakes were highly efficient at high alpha, rendering the aircraft safe and easy to fly.

The MiG-29 made use of composites and aluminum-lithium alloys to cut airframe weight. The elevated position of the cockpit and the bubble canopy with one-piece windscreen offered excellent all-round visibility for the pilot. This was further helped by the triple rear-view mirrors on the windscreen frame. The pilot sat on a "Zvezda" (Star) K-36DM zero-zero ejection seat.

The definitive MiG-29 had a length of 15.0 m (49 ft 2.55 in.) less pitot boom, a wingspan of 10.8 m (35 ft 5.19 in.), a wing area of 38.0 m² (408.6 sq. ft), and a height on ground of 4.56 m (14 ft 11.52 in.).

Empty weight was 9,670 kg (21,318 lbs) and normal takeoff weight with a 3,650-kg (8,046-lb) internal fuel load was 13,570 kg (29,916 lbs). Takeoff thrust-to-weight ratio was 1.23, and specific wing loading was 350 kg/m² (1,706 lb/sq. ft).

Unlike the Su-27, the MiG-29 operated mostly over friendly territory, venturing only some 100 km (55 nm) beyond the frontlines. The highly effective K-27, K-73, and K-14 new-generation AAMs and twin-barrel 30-mm gun enabled the MiG-29 to destroy highly maneuverable targets within a broad speed and altitude range.

The SOR stated the MiG-29's primary roles as counter-air and top cover for ground troops. The CAS/strike role was viewed as secondary, which Mikoyan admitted was a big mistake. The aircraft was required to have a top speed of 2,500 km/h (1,388 kts) at high altitude, 1,500 km/h (833 kts) at sea level. It was to go from 600 to 1,100 km/h (333 to 611 kts) in 13 seconds, and from 1,100 to 1,300 km/h (722 kts) in 7 seconds. Service ceiling with 50% fuel was 19,500 m (63,976 ft); maximum rate of climb at 1,000 m (3,280 ft) was 325 m/sec (1,066 ft/sec). Range was 800 km (444 nm) at S/L and 2,750 km (1,527 nm) at high altitude with a single 1,500-lit. (33 Imp. gal.) drop-tank on the fuselage centerline. The aircraft was stressed for nine Gs. Combined with the high alpha limit, broad speed and altitude range, high thrust-to-weight ratio, and carefully designed aerodynamics-enhanced flight safety, this allowed prolonged violent maneuvering in combat.

The definitive version of the MiG-29 advanced development project was examined and approved when the first prototype was actually flying.

DEVELOPMENT
2

MiG-29 Prototypes and Pre-production Aircraft (901 to 904, 908 and 917 to 925)

Originally, the Mikoyan OKB planned to build 25 flying prototypes and a number of static test airframes. The unusually large number of development aircraft was due to the extreme complexity of the flight-test program; performance and handling, avionics, armament trials, etc., had to be assigned to different aircraft. For the first time in Mikoyan's design practice, a full-scale aircraft would be tested in the TsAGI wind tunnel and special airframes built for avionics trials and avionics compatibility testing.

In keeping with the original two-stage development, the development aircraft was earmarked for completion to MiG-29A standards with the SUV-23ML-2 WCS. It soon turned out, however, that the radar set of the Yantar (Sapfeer-23ML-2) radar did not fit the MiG-29 airframe. Making the LERXes slightly thicker cured the problem by providing more room in the avionics bay.

As a result of the 1976 cancellation, the MiG-29A airframes (aircraft 905 through 907 and 909 through 916) were never built. The code number "908," originally allocated

Aircraft 901 was the first MiG-29 flying prototype. The nose gear is well forward and was later moved to reduce intake FOD ingestion. (RSK MiG archive)

Another view of the Aircraft 901. Note the landing lights that fold out of the main gear wheel wells. (RSK MiG archive)

A front view of the first prototype. Given the change in wing leading-edge outside the root extensions, it is easy to see where the swing-wing impression originated. (RSK MiG archive)

Aircraft 901 shows the large FOD guard on the nosewheel, the familiar side profile, and the all-moving stabilators. (RSK MiG archive)

to a MiG-29A, was later reused for a powerplant development aircraft built to replace the third prototype, which crashed during trials. Thus only 14 flight-test aircraft were actually built.

In 1977 the first prototype rolled out and ground systems tests commenced. Mikoyan engineers incorporated excessive structural strength in the MiG-29, making the aircraft over-

weight. For the first time in Soviet fighter design practice, a service life limit had been set. As a result, measures were taken to reduce stress buildup in the fighter's structural elements. Both VIAM and TsAGI expressly recommended the use of composites, and Mikoyan had high hopes, expecting to save some 400 kg (881 lbs) of airframe weight by using them. The real weight saving, howev-

er, was only about 200 kg (440 lbs). As a result, the first prototype's TOW was 700 kg (1,543 lbs) above the specified limit.

On October 6, 1977, the MiG-29 became airborne for the first time with Mikoyan chief test pilot Aleksandr V. Fedotov at the controls. The three prototypes followed the trials program until spring 1981. The first prototype was used to evaluate per-

Starting a four-year flight trials program, the MiG-29 takes off on its first flight on October 6, 1977, with Aleksander V. Fedotov at the controls. (still from a Mikoyan video)

This is the only known photo of the second prototype, Aircraft 902. The first to have integral wing fuel tanks, it was the natural choice for explosive tests under fire after 229 test flights. (Yefim Gordon archive)

formance and handling as well as measure airframe loads. Fedotov began low-speed handling and stalling/spinning trials as early as 1978. Ventral fins were added to all prototypes to improve directional stability at high alpha and to facilitate spin recovery.

Early test flights revealed the location of the nose-gear unit was such that any debris flung up by the nosewheels flew into the air intakes. Since the MiG-29 had the "patented" FOD protection doors, this didn't seem to matter much, and the nose-gear unit was left as it was. The first prototype was retired in Zhukovskiy after making 230 flights. Years later it was donated to the VVS Museum in Monino southeast of Moscow.

Construction of the second and third prototypes (902 and 903) started simultaneously, but the latter aircraft was actually completed first. Initially, aircraft 902 was identical to the first prototype, but before it was completed the nose-gear unit was shortened slightly and moved aft 1.5 m (4 ft 11 in.) to further reduce the risk of foreign object ingestion. The second prototype (902) – which was actually the *third* flight-test article – entered flight tests in November 1979, making seven flights before year-end; three more by

March 15, 1980. It had no radar and was therefore used to verify the opto-electronic targeting/navigation system. This aircraft was also the first to have integral wing fuel tanks.

It was soon discovered that the aircraft's AOA limit was 5° lower than specified, as violent vibration was encountered at high alpha. The cause of the trouble was traced to sections of the leading-edge flaps; this gave a weight saving of 15 kg (33 lbs) but created turbulence. After making 229 test flights, the aircraft was relegated to the aircraft systems test facility in Faustovo near Moscow. There it was first used to test the fire suppression system, and later fired upon to check if the fuel tanks would explode.

The third prototype (903) was rolled out ahead of the second one and made its first flight in June 1978. Serving for engine testing, its career proved to be extremely short. On June 15 the aircraft crashed on its ninth flight when one of the engines suffered an uncontained compressor failure and fragments severed the control runs.

The fourth prototype (904) was intended mainly for dynamic load measurement and equipped with numerous stress sensors. It took to the air on May 15, 1979. After mak-

ing 40 flights within the manufacturer's flight-test program in July 1981, the aircraft was handed over to LII. LII representatives, however, tell a different story, claiming that it made only 11 flights with Mikoyan before being transferred to LII and making another 148 flights there.

Engine testing continued with the fifth prototype (908), which made its first flight on April 5, 1979. This aircraft fared little better than its predecessor, however. It was lost on its 48th flight on October 31, 1980, when a combustion chamber failed; the resulting fire burned through control runs and the aircraft dived into the ground.

Aircraft 901, 903, and 908 took part only in manufacturer's trials; the other prototypes were used in the state acceptance trials. In the course of the tests, the fighter was modified to incorporate the GSh-301 single-barrel 30-mm gun.

The sixth prototype, aircraft 917, was the standard-setter for the production MiG-29 and incorporated various improvements. This aircraft later became the first MiG-29 to feature the extended-chord rudders protruding beyond the fin trailing edge, a characteristic of late-production MiG-29 aircraft. It was first flown in December 1979, and was used in the aerodynamics research trials and tested for performance and handling, making a total of 369 test flights.

The seventh development aircraft (918) was the first MiG-29 prototype to have a fire-control radar but no optoelectronic targeting system. It first flew on May 22, 1980, and made 265 flights (including 163 flights within the WCS test program), gaining the distinction of the type's first air-to-air "kill" with a K-27R IR-homing missile. In 1982 aircraft 918 was modified under the MiG-29K shipboard fighter program with an arrestor hook added under the aft fuselage and was unofficially designated MiG-29KVP (as described in detail later).

Under the state acceptance trials program, the prototypes made 331 test flights between them by the end of 1980. The intensity of the trials increased when four more single-seaters (919, 920, 921, and 923) and the prototype of the MiG-29UB train-

The fourth prototype was used to look into the possibility of using the MiG-29 as a fighter-bomber and is shown here with weapons installed. The gap between the parallel engines is readily apparent. (Yefim Gordon archive)

The fourth prototype, Aircraft 904, was mainly for dynamic load measurement; therefore it was fitted with numerous stress sensors. It was withdrawn from the program in 1991 before preservation in Moscow. (Yefim Gordon archive)

Aircraft 917, the 17th flight-test aircraft, is seen here after modification with extended-chord rudders to improve the MiG-29's directional control; these were a late addition during flight tests. The dorsal strakes on the upper wing surfaces incorporated the IRCM flare dispensers, but were deleted in the later models. (RSK MiG archive)

er (951) joined the program in 1981. By the end of the year, the total number of test flights had increased to 700 (647 for the singles and 53 for the two-seat).

Aircraft 919, which first flew on July 30, 1981, was another radar test vehicle. Unlike 918, it featured the new Ts100 digital computer, replacing the "Orbita-20" analog computer. In July 1985, after making 266 flights with Mikoyan, it was transferred to LII, which investigated the effect of vibration and high temperatures on the aircraft systems. It was also used to examine the effect of G loads on gun and missile firing. It was retired in 1991 after 364 flights.

The ninth aircraft (920), used for avionics compatibility testing, was the first to feature a complete set of mission avionics. It entered flight test on March 6, 1981. After making 373 flights it went to the nuclear test range on the Novaya Zemlya archipelago in the Barents Sea (probably to test its tactical nuclear weapons delivery capability).

Engine testing was finally completed on the tenth aircraft (921) that first flew on August 21, 1981; this included investigating the effect of gun firing and missile launches on engine operation. After making 376 flights under the MiG-29's flight-test program, it found further use as a testbed for the uprated RD-33K engine developed for the vastly upgraded MiG-29M version. The air-

Aircraft 919 is on display in the city park in Zhukovskiy on Aviation Day (August 16, 1988). This is traditionally the third Sunday in August. Both 918 and 919 were radar test vehicles, 919 having the new Ts100 digital computer. (Yefim Gordon)

craft survives at Mikoyan's test facility at LII, Zhukovskiy.

Aircraft 922 joined the test program on May 20, 1982, but it was withdrawn from use after four flights, including three for WCS testing. It was then handed over to TsAGI for wind tunnel tests.

The next development aircraft (923) made its first flight in Zhukovskiy on November 4, 1981. It was soon ferried to NII VVS in Akhtoobinsk for testing of the opto-electronic targeting/navigation system and internal gun.

Aircraft 924 was rolled out on September 30, 1981, but it did not make its first flight until September 9, 1983. On December 29, 1983, after 22 flights, it was transferred to LII. The institute used it for dynamic load measurement and later for evaluating modified engine nozzles and air intakes. On August 18, 1991 – one day before the notorious military *coup d'é- tat* that brought an end to the existence of the Soviet Union – the aircraft was placed in the Aviation Day static display in front of TsAGI's administrative building at Zhukovskiy.

The fourteenth and final development aircraft (925) was the definitive standard-setter for full-scale production, incorporating all changes. It flew for the first time on December 30, 1982, making 235 test flights before it was withdrawn from use at LII. It was used, among other things, to check the interaction between the fire-control radar and the IRST. The next year the MiG-29 entered production at MMZ No. 30 under the in-house designation 9.12.

Improvements started coming as soon as the first fighters rolled off the production line at Khodyn- ka. Operational experience in Afghanistan, where the Mujahideen guerrillas were widely using portable IR-homing surface-to-air missiles such as Stinger and Redeye,

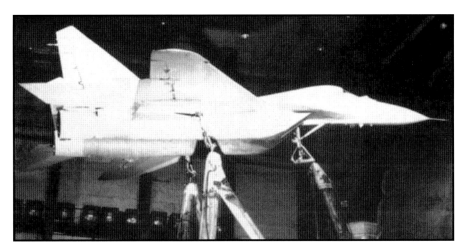

Aircraft 922 gets tested in the TsAGI T-101 wind tunnel in Zhukovskiy. This spectacular wind tunnel is a major design tool at the Central Aerodynamics & Hydrodynamics Institute. (Yefim Gordon archive)

forced the engineers to devise counter-measures. Thus the MiG-29 received infrared countermeasures (IRCM) flare dispensers, initially located on the wings ahead of the fin fillets. The arrangement was tested on the sixth prototype. Dorsal strakes of varying length incorporating the chaff/flare dispensers were tested during the long program. Eventually, the dispensers were fitted flush with the rear fuselage skin on the MiG-29K and MiG-29M. The final pre-production aircraft also participated in IRCM testing.

Fedotov investigated the MiG-29's spinning characteristics. It transpired that if you really wanted the MiG-29 to spin you had to forcibly keep it in that position – the aircraft simply would not spin of its own accord! When the pilot let go of the controls after initiating a spin, the fighter recovered automatically. On the minus side, high-alpha handling posed some problems. The MiG-29 was found to have reverse roll reaction to rudder input at high AOAs – that is, if the pilot applied right rudder, the aircraft rolled to the left instead of to the right. Conversely, the fighter behaved normally if bank was countered by rudder input. This "quirk" initially caused the AOA to be limited to 20°. AOA was later increased to 22°, then 24°, etc., as tests progressed.

The West got news of the MiG-29's existence in the spring of 1979 when a US surveillance satellite photographed a prototype on LII's airfield in Zhukovskiy. The manufacturer was unknown at the time, so the aircraft received the provisional reporting name *Ram-L*, because at that time Zhukovskiy was erroneously referred to as Ramenskoye. By 1982, when the true designation became known, the MiG-29 was allocated the ASCC reporting name Fulcrum. Provisional three-view drawings published in 1982 were wildly inaccurate.

The rear portion of Aircraft 924 was used to test modified engine intakes and nozzles. The so-called "turkey feathers" of unequal length are easily seen. (Aleksey Mikheyev)

This is the first photograph of the MiG-29 from space, made by the Pentagon in 1979. The name "Fulcrum" was allocated after this event, but inaccurate drawings were still circulating in 1982. (Flight International)

This is a photo of the K-77 (RVV-AE) air-to-air medium-range missile tests from Aircraft 919. The same aircraft had achieved its first kill on a remote-controlled MiG-21 target drone with a K-73. (Yefim Gordon archive)

MiG-29 3 Variants

Fulcrum-A, MiG-29 Tactical Fighter (*izdeliye* 9.12)

Many enterprises in the aerospace, electronics, defense, and other industries supplied components for the MiG-29. The production run was split into batches of at least fifteen aircraft. Like the prototypes, the first 70 aircraft had ventral fins outboard of the engine nacelles. By 1984, however, the automatic bank corrector in the rudder control circuit passed its trials and was introduced on production aircraft, rendering these fins unnecessary. Most early production aircraft removed them in service. The AOA limit set by the manufacturer was 26°. However, in service the VVS imposed a 24° limit just to be safe.

Soon after production entry, the MiG-29 was equipped with BVP-30-26M chaff/flare dispensers ahead of the fins, with thirty 26-mm (1.02-in.) infared countermeasures (IRCM) flares each. A vortex generator was added to the pitot boom, similar to the final version of the MiG-23MLD Flogger-K.

Many composite structures were built into the early airframes, but riveting problems and structural failures plagued the system. In the end only the composite fins and access panels were retained.

The MiG-29 (9.12) had an internal fuel capacity of 4,300 lit. (946 Imp. gal.); the fuel was carried in four fuselage integral tanks and two wing tanks. A 1,520-lit. (334.4 Imp. gal.) drop-tank could be carried on the centerline. Unlike most Soviet fighters, the Fulcrum's was semi-conformal. The bulky drop-tank obstructed the APU exhaust, which was located between the engine nacelles. To correct this, Mikoyan incorporated a unique feature – the tank had a straight-through vertical duct or "pipe" at the rear enabling the APU to exhaust right through it!

Fulcrum-B, MiG-29UB Conversion Trainer (*izdeliye* 9.51 or *izdeliye* 30)

The Mikoyan OKB developed a combat-capable trainer version of the fighter designated MiG-29UB. A tandem cockpit enclosed by a common, aft-hinged canopy gave shorter ejection time in emergencies. To avoid a major redesign and ensure maximum commonality with the single-seat, the fire-control radar was

The MiG-29 production line at Lookhovitsy. Note the aircraft are on their undercarriages at an early stage and are loosely positioned on the shop floor with fairly lightweight, easily movable assembly gantries.

deleted, leaving only the IRST and HMS; thus the R-27R medium-range AAM with SARH was excluded from the MiG-29UB's weapons range.

Despite the lack of radar, the MiG-29UB retained dogfighting and strike capability, as the IRST could engage targets at 25-30 km (13-16 nm) range. Special emulators were fitted to allow pilots to train in on intercept techniques, using the radar, firing SARH missiles, and dealing with systems failures. The aircraft featured data recorders for mission analysis. It was designed to operate in visual and instrumental meteorological conditions, day and night, enabling rapid transition to the single-seat MiG-29.

The MiG-29UB prototype first flew on April 29, 1981. It made 53 flights that year. The second prototype was used in the state acceptance trials program. The third stayed with Mikoyan for demonstrations. After successfully passing the manufacturer's flight tests and state acceptance trials, the MiG-29UB entered production at the Gor'kiy aircraft factory No. 21. "Assembly" would be more accurate, since the main airframe components were manufactured in Moscow and shipped in for final assembly and equipment installation.

In VVS documents, the MiG-29UB was referred to as *izdeliye* 30. The trainer's NATO code name was Fulcrum-B, the single-seater (9.12) becoming the Fulcrum-*A*.

Newly completed MiG-29s sit in the final assembly shop of the Lookhovitsy Mechanical Plant. Many built airframes were stored here after orders were reduced in the 1990s. (Yefim Gordon)

An early production MiG-29. Note the centerline fuel tank mounted between the engines. (RSK MiG archive)

This early MiG-29 had the ventral fins characteristic of the initial production version. (Viktor Drushlyakov)

Fulcrum-A, MiG-29, Export Version A (*izdeliye* 9.12A)

Soon after the initial production version became operational with the VVS, the factory began manufacturing a slightly downgraded export version intended for the Warsaw Pact countries. Known as 9.12A, "export version A" stayed in production from 1988 to 1991 and was supplied to Bulgaria, Czechoslovakia, East Germany, Poland, and Romania.

Fulcrum-A, MiG-29, Export Version B (*izdeliye* 9.12B)

An even more downgraded export version designated 9.12B was developed for "friendly" states outside the Warsaw Pact. This aircraft entered production in 1986 and was supplied to Hungary, India, Iraq, Syria, and some other states.

Fulcrum-C, MiG-29 Tactical Fighter (*izdeliye* 9.13)

One of the biggest problems facing the designers of Soviet fourth-generation fighters was meeting the specified range requirements. The advanced development project specified a range of 800 km (444 nm) at S/L and 2,750 km (1,527 nm) at high altitude with one centerline drop-tank. In reality, it was 700 km (388 nm) and 2,100 km (1,166 nm), respectively, for the production MiG-29.

Only the No. 1 fuselage tank in the spine could be readily enlarged, increasing capacity by 240 lit. (52.8 Imp. gal.) and giving it an internal fuel volume of 4,540 lit. (998.8 Imp. gal.). As the next-best solution, the engineers introduced "wet" wing pylons, permitting the carriage of two 1,150-lit. (253 Imp. gal.) drop-tanks. Fitting three drop-tanks increased the total fuel volume to 8,340 lit. (1,834.8 Imp. gal.), providing a ferry range of 3,000 km (1,666 nm).

The ECM suite also took longer to develop than anticipated; late MiG-29s were to feature an L-203B jammer in the avionics bay aft of the cockpit. Along with the enlarged No. 1 fuel tank, this required a change in the fuselage spine shape. The upper fuselage contour became convex instead of concave, giving the fighter a distinctive appearance and earning it the nickname *"gorbahtyy"* – "hunchback." The ECM aerials were located under four prominent dielectric panels at the wingtips to give 360° coverage.

In 1983 the Mikoyan OKB converted three standard Batch 4 aircraft into prototypes of the new version. Trials began in April 1984, with the three prototypes making more than 400 flights between them. Production lasted from 1986

Three initial-production MiG-29s take flight from the Kubinka AFB regiment. Kubinka is the premier Russian military base, similar in status to Nellis AFB, Nevada. (Yefim Gordon archive)

Mikoyan retained MiG-29 (izdeliye 9.12) numbered 10 Blue *for demonstration and training purposes. This probably explains the immaculate paint scheme. (RSK MiG archive)*

10 Blue is training here over what might be termed a fair-weather landscape for central Russia. This aircraft crashed at Le Bourget at the 1989 Paris Air Show. (RSK MiG archive)

to 1991. Fulcrum-A production continued in parallel on a small scale, mainly for export. The first production 9.13 was the standard-setter for the production Fulcrum-C, incorporating all the refinements. This aircraft made more than 500 test flights at GLITs until the program was completed in November 1988. It was donated to the Great Patriotic War Museum in Moscow.

The first production "fatbacks" were deployed in East Germany. The new version promptly attracted the attention of Western military intelligence and received the reporting name Fulcrum-C.

Fulcrum-C, MiG-29 Experimental Fighter (*izdeliye* 9.14)

In 1984 the Mikoyan OKB developed a version of the MiG-29 with an enhanced WCS including a "Ryabina" low-light-level TV/laser designator pod. The weapons range was expanded to include *Zvezda* Kh-25M (AS-10 *Karen*) and *Spetstekhnika* Kh-29 (AS-14 *Kedge*) TV-guided or laser-guided air-to-ground missiles and KAB-500 "smart bombs." The maximum bomb load was 4,500 kg (9,920 lbs) with eight bombs on MERs under the wings and one on the fuselage centerline.

The prototype was a converted Fulcrum-A. It first flew on February 13, 1985. The Ryabina LLLTV/laser designator system was still under development, so the aircraft served to test the augmented bomb armament and examine the possibility of operations from dirt strips. Later it was used in the MiG-29S upgrade program. It participated in several international air shows in 1991-92.

However, 9.14 never entered production because in the mid 1980s the Mikoyan OKB began working on a major upgrade of the Fulcrum, the MiG-29M, which also had pinpoint strike capability. The prototype remained a one-off and is still operational at GLITs in Akhtoobinsk, with more than 800 flights to its credit.

Testbeds and Research Aircraft

a) "Aircraft 970" and "Aircraft 971" Weapons Testbeds

These two production Fulcrum-As had a modified WCS, serving as weapons with the "Vympel" weapons design bureau. They were used to test medium-range AAMs. The first aircraft took off in May 1985 and the second in January 1986. The program finished in August 1989 and included missile separation safety trials in all

Two views of a standard production MiG-29 Fulcrum-A (izdeliye 9.12) demonstrate that the straight leading edges on the stabilators and the genuine dorsal intake louvers are clearly visible in the plan view. (Yefim Gordon archive)

Blue 51, the first prototype MiG-29UB combat trainer, flies overhead during flight tests. Note the photo-theodolite markings are clearly visible. (Yefim Gordon archive)

This MiG-29UB prototype sits in the shop of Mikoyan design bureau, 1980. Only the fire-control radar was deleted in the trainer version, thereby retaining most of the combat capability. (RSK MiG archive)

flight modes, verification of changes to the N-019 radar, and live firing trials against La-17M, M-21, and Tu-16M Badger target drones.

b) MiG-29 Stealth Technology Testbed

To investigate ways of reducing the aircraft's radar signature, a standard-production MiG-29 was coated experimentally with a radar-absorbent material (RAM). Trials showed that the RAM significantly reduced the fighter's radar cross-section (RCS).

c) Uprated RD-33 (izdeliye 21) Engine Testbed

After completing its State acceptance trials program, the tenth MiG-29 prototype was converted into a testbed for a version of the RD-33K engine

uprated to 8,800 kgp (19,400 lb st) in full afterburner. This was developed for the upgraded MiG-29M. The prototype engine was installed in only the fighter's port nacelle. The air intakes were converted to MiG-29M standards, with downward-hinging FOD protection grilles downstream instead of solid doors at the mouth and no auxiliary dorsal intakes.

d) MiG-29KVP

In 1982, when the N-019 radar had passed its trials, the eighth prototype was converted under the MiG-29K program. The objective was to test the type's compatibility with a conventional takeoff and landing (CTOL) aircraft carrier and perfect carrier operations techniques. Unneces-

sary equipment was removed, resulting in a gross weight of only 12 tons (26,455 lbs). An arrestor hook was fitted under the aft fuselage and the airframe was reinforced. The aircraft was unofficially designated MiG-29KVP.

Carrier operations trials proceeded at Novofyodorovka airbase near the city of Saki in the Crimea, home to the AV-MF Flight Test Centre. A special "unsinkable carrier" had been built there, featuring a ski jump and an arrestor system. On August 21, 1982, Aviard G. Fastovets made the first takeoff from the provisional T-1 ski jump (T = *tramplin*). The aircraft became airborne at 240 km/h (133 kts) after a 250 m (820 ft) takeoff run. Between October 1 and October 25, 1984, the MiG-29KVP

The first prototype MiG-29UB still survives at Mikoyan's flight-test facility in Zhukovskiy, albeit sans engines. The family resemblances to the Flogger and Foxhound are noticeable in the background. (Yefim Gordon)

Side view of a standard-production MiG-29UB Fulcrum-B (izdeliye 9.51). The common canopy speeds up the ejection process for both pilots in case of an emergency. (Yefim Gordon archive)

This production MiG-29 (11 Blue, "Aircraft 211") was used by Mikoyan for research. Note the additional pitot heads on the forward fuselage. (Viktor Drushlyakov)

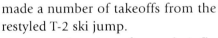

MiG-29 No971 testbed was used for RVV-AE missiles trials. Note the leading-edge slats deployed in this photo. (RSK MiG archive)

MiG-29 Fulcrum-A weapons: B-8M1 rocket pods, KMGU packs, fuel drop-tanks, 250-kg and 500-kg bombs, R-27R, R-73, and R-60 AAMs. The curved wing profile is readily apparent. (Yefim Gordon)

made a number of takeoffs from the restyled T-2 ski jump.

Later the aircraft was briefly used as an instructional airframe by the Moscow Energy Institute before being donated to the VVS Museum in Monino.

e) "Aircraft 211" (izdeliye 9.21)

In the late 1970s and early 1980s, GosNIIAS began examining the possibilities of integrating digital avionics into the MiG-29. The BTsK-29 digital avionics suite enabled multiplex data exchange, thus significantly enhancing combat potential. To this end an early production MiG-29 was converted into an avionics testbed in late 1987. Flight tests began in April 1988 but were soon suspended.

f) Equipment Reliability Research Aircraft

After completing an equipment reliability test program on "919," LII began further research in order to deal with the MiG-29's teething troubles. The research aircraft was a standard-production Fulcrum-A borrowed from the Air Force combat training centre in Lipetsk. This aircraft later became Mikoyan's demonstrator workhorse, eventually crashing at the 1989 Paris air show.

g) N-010 Radar Testbed (izdeliye 9.16)

A production "fatback" MiG-29 was converted into an avionics testbed for the Phazotron N-010 "Zhuk" radar developed for the MiG-29M. It made the first post-conversion flight

on January 12, 1987, but trials had to be suspended after radar failure. When it was repaired, the aircraft went to Akhtoobinsk and remained operational there until 1990.

MiG-29S Tactical Fighter (izdeliye 9.13S), Fulcrum-C

In the late 1980s, Mikoyan conducted additional research in order to adapt the new R-77 active radar homing missile to the Fulcrum. The result was an upgraded version of the Fulcrum-C, designated MiG-29S. It could guide missiles to two targets at a time and operated in concert with R-27RE and R-77 AAMs.

Modifications to the control system increased the fighter's maximum

AOA to 28°. The airframe was reinforced, permitting an increase in MTOW to 20,000 kg (44,091 lbs). The ordnance load in the strike role was increased to 4,000 kg (8,818 lbs) of bombs on four MERs under the wings (two 500-kg/1,102-lb bombs per station). Like the standard Fulcrum-C, the MiG-29S had provisions for three drop-tanks.

By Mikoyan estimates, the new missiles increased the fighter's combat efficiency 2.5 to 3 times. In a long-range "missile duel," the MiG-29S had 10% better chances than the F-16C and Rafale, and 25% better chances than the Gripen and Mirage 2000-5.

Three Fulcrum-C prototypes were modified in 1988 and 1989, respectively, to integrate the R-77 AAM with the new radar. The first "real" prototype entered flight test on December 23, 1990. When the trials program was completed, VVS aircraft overhaul plant at Kubinka AB began upgrading early-production Fulcrum-A/Cs to MiG-29S standard.

Fulcrum-A, MiG-29S Tactical Fighter (*izdeliye* 9.12S)

A similar upgrade of the original production version, Fulcrum-A, quite logically bore the same service designation, MiG-29S; however, the manufacturer's designation was different – 9.12S. Outwardly, the aircraft differed from the version described above in having the original concave fuselage

These two views are of a standard production MiG-29 Fulcrum-C (izdeliye 9.13). The need for increased range meant increasing the size of the main dorsal fuel tank, creating the concave "fatback" profile common to and further enlarged in subsequent models. (Yefim Gordon archive)

spine. Thus, it had less internal fuel and lacked the L203B jammer. Four were retained by MAPO-MiG for air show demonstration purposes and painted in a metallic green/blue/silver camouflage.

Fulcrum-A, MiG-29SD Export Version (*izdeliye* 9.12SD)

Predictably, an export version of the "skinny" MiG-29S (9.12S) appeared before long under the designation MiG-29SD ("D" stands for *dozaprahvka* – refueling). It featured an RLPK-29ME (export) radar targeting system (N-019ME radar) and an OEPrNK-29-1E optoelectronic targeting/navigation system offering a major improvement in combat capabilities over the standard export Fulcrum. Western avionics were optional.

Malaysia was the launch customer, and the aircraft entered production in 1995, sometimes identified as MiG-29N. These have Western tactical navigation equipment (TACAN), VOR/ILS, IFF and ATC transponders, additional HF and UHF radios, and other avionics. The flight instruments are marked in feet and knots.

The upgraded WCS enabled the MiG-29SD to engage two aerial targets at one time, firing two missiles consecutively or simultaneously; target lock-on occurred manually or automatically. A hose-and-drogue aerial refueling system with a strap-on refueling probe was developed for the MiG-29SD to be fitted at customer request; this was tested on Fulcrum-A 357 Blue.

Fulcrum-C, MiG-29SE Export Version (*izdeliye* 9.13SE)

A similar export version of the "fatback" MiG-29S was designated MiG-29SE ("E" for export). It differed

These three views show a production MiG-29 Fulcrum-C with four R-73 short-range AAMs. Wet-wing pylons were also added to allow a carriage of two 1,150-liter drop-tanks. (Yefim Gordon)

357 Blue, the MiG-29 refueling system demonstrator, sits proudly on display at the ILA airshow in Berlin. (Yefim Gordon)

Non-flying Aircraft 925 was converted to represent the original version of the MiG-29SMT project, seen here at LII in December 1997. (Yefim Gordon)

The second prototype MiG-29SMT, during trials, shows the new dorsal profile caused by additional fuel tanks. (Yefim Gordon)

The second prototype MiG-29SMT, 917 Blue, is pictured here with two Kh-31P anti-radiation missiles. The maximum ordnance load of the SMT is 4,000 kg. (Yefim Gordon)

from the MiG-29SD only in having a bigger internal fuel capacity.

MiG-29SM Multi-Role Fighter

To enhance the Fulcrum's strike capability, the MiG-29S was developed into the MiG-29SM (*modernizeerovannyy* – upgraded). It could carry Kh-29T TV-guided AGMs and KAB-500KR TV-guided bombs. The weapon projected a "bomb's eye view" to a display in the cockpit, enabling the pilot to hit targets with pinpoint accuracy. The ordnance load was 4,000 kg (8,818 lbs). In production form the MiG-29SM had flight refueling capability with a fully retractable L-shaped probe. Mikoyan estimated the modification would triple the combat potential compared to 9.12.

MiG-29 Refueling System Testbed

The Malaysian contract signed on June 7, 1994 stated that 14 out of 16 Fulcrums ordered by TUDM (i.e., all of the single-seat MiG-29SDs) were to be retrofitted with refueling probes upon completion of deliveries. To this end a standard-production MiG-29 (9.12) was converted into a testbed for the optional refueling probe developed for the MiG-29SD/SE/SM.

MiG-29SMT Multi-Role Fighter (*izdeliye* 9.17)

Operational experience with the MiG-29 proved that it had better maneuverability, speed, and service ceiling than the best Western fighters in its class. Range, on the other hand, was inadequate. This led MAPO-MiG to begin a radical upgrade in 1997.

Designated 9.17, the new version was based on the "fatback" MiG-29S. In its original form, the air intakes were borrowed straight from the

MiG-29M, with FOD protection grilles replacing the earlier solid doors. The upper auxiliary intakes were deleted, making room for 930 lit. (204.6 Imp. gal.) extra fuel in the LERXes. The forward fuselage was identical to the MiG-29M's, featuring a raised cockpit and options for a refueling probe.

The spine was even fatter than on the Fulcrum-C, increasing avionics bay volume by 500 lit. (110 Imp. gal.). It incorporated two strap-on fuel tanks, a MiG-29M-style dorsal airbrake, and a MiG-29M-style boat-tail fairing between the engine nozzles. The wings were modified to incorporate four hardpoints each and hold 390 lit. (85.8 Imp. gal.) extra fuel. The fighter had increased-area stabilators with dogtooth and broader-chord fin root sections, again from the MiG-29M. The main gear units were beefed up. Fuselage integral tank No. 3 was also reinforced and enlarged by 200 lit. (44 Imp. gal.); additionally, the aircraft could carry enlarged drop-tanks under the wings and had provisions for a fully retractable MiG-29K-style refueling probe.

Aircraft 9.17 received the official designation MiG-29SMT, the "T" denoting *toplivo* (fuel) and referring to the increased fuel load. In late 1997, however, the engineers changed the project considerably – not least because MAPO objected to such drastic structural changes. The main problem was that the complicated redesign of the air intakes was not worth the effort, giving only a slight increase in fuel capacity.

In autumn 1997, one of GLITs' former Fulcrum-Cs was modified by Mikoyan and put through trials under the MiG-29SMT program. The conversion concerned only the cockpit equipped with an EFIS to MiG-29SMT standard to improve flight and target data presentation.

The cockpit of the MiG-29SMT-I shows the two large color-screen displays. (Yefim Gordon)

The cockpit of the upgraded MiG-29SMT-II features the new navigation suite with ring laser gyros, on board INS, and satellite link. (Yefim Gordon)

On April 22, 1998, the MiG-29SMT was again unveiled to aviation dignitaries and the aviation press at Mikoyan's flight-test facility in Zhukovskiy. This time, however, it was the real thing, and it was far different from the November 1997 mockup. Since then, the aircraft had been extensively modified to bring it,

externally at least, to MiG-29SMT standards with a more convex upper fuselage, extended MiG-29M-style "beaver tail," and one-piece dorsal airbrake. The MiG-29SMT made its first flight that day.

The second prototype, a converted late-production Fulcrum-C, entered flight test on November 28,

1997. In March 1998 the aircraft was turned over to Mikoyan's experimental shop for complete conversion to MiG-29SMT standards, becoming the first "true" MiG-29SMT. On December 29, 1998, the first "production" MiG-29SMT was delivered to Zhukovskiy. As mentioned earlier, the MiG-29SMT can fill the strike, interceptor, tactical reconnaissance, and tactical airborne command-post roles. Experts claim the fighter's combat potential is eight times that of the baseline MiG-29 Fulcrum-A, while direct operating costs are 35-40% lower.

New avionics enable the MiG-29SMT Stage I to carry all kinds of aircraft weapons, including Western missiles. Each of the fighter's seven computers equals ten computers fitted to 1982 standard-production MiG-29s. Using modern electronic components produced a weight saving of some 600 kg (1,322 lbs).

MiG-29UBT Combat Trainer

In the summer of 1998, Mikoyan's experimental shop began converting a MiG-29UB Fulcrum-B combat trainer into the prototype MiG-29UBT. The MiG-29UBT featured increased fuel capacity in a bulged fuselage spine *à la* MiG-29SMT and updated avionics, including "glass cockpits." The "fatback" trainer entered flight test on August 25, 1998.

MiG-29MF Multi-Role Fighter (Proposal)

In 1997 Russia began negotiations with the Philippines, offering the MiG-29 to the Philippine Air Force. This version is called MiG-29MF by Mikoyan.

These three views of the MiG-29SMT 01 Blue (c/n 2960720165), completed in the last days of 1998, came as a welcome gift to the Russian AF. The volume of the additional dorsal fuel-tanks enables a major range improvement without compromising the streamlining. (Yefim Gordon)

Unlike the basic MiG-29UB, the MiG-29UBT had full combat capability with three screens in the rear glass-cockpit, and an upgraded WCS. (Yefim Gordon)

The second prototype of the MiG-29UBT, 52 Blue, was the first two-seat aircraft to feature a flight refueling capability. (Yefim Gordon)

The MiG-29SMT 01 Blue rests with the second prototype of the MiG-29UBT at Zhukovskiy. (Yefim Gordon)

This MiG-29 Fulcrum-C test aircraft has special anti-radar coating. This stealth technology testbed confirmed that the RAM coating significantly reduced the RCS. Similar experiments were tried with the Su-25 Frogfoot. (Yefim Gordon)

THE UPGRADE

MiG-29M Multi-Role Fighter (*izdeliye* 9.15)

As far back as the late 1970s, Mikoyan started looking for ways to enhance the MiG-29's combat potential. Thus began a new development stage that resulted in what could be called the second-generation Fulcrum – the MiG-29M (*modernizeerovannyy* – upgraded).

The main objectives were versatility, longer range, and reduced losses in action. While primarily similar to the basic MiG-29, the MiG-29M featured aerodynamic refinements, improved handling, stability, and technological changes, making it easier to build. The result was, in effect, a new aircraft so different from the basic MiG-29 that it was to be placed in a new category – the so-called "generation 4+" multi-role fighters.

To power the MiG-29M, the Klimov OKB developed a "landlubber" version of the RD-33K engine (*izdeliye* 21) designed for the MiG-29K shipboard fighter (see next chapter). The new engine had a duplex full-authority digital engine-control (FADEC) system, a duplex automatic fuel flow management system, and a new accessory gearbox. Besides having greater reliability, the FADEC produced increased acceleration.

The MiG-29M featured redesigned air intakes. The solid FOD protection doors and dorsal auxiliary intakes of the Fulcrum-A/B/C were removed and replaced by downward-hinging grids further downstream. The walls of the main wheel wells were perforated to admit additional air when the grids were up. The intakes had a lower lip that could be deflected 20° down to improve engine operation at high alpha; the FADEC controlled these and the intake ramps.

Major changes were made to the airframe. Most of it, especially the forward fuselage, was made of 01420 aluminum-lithium (Al-Li) alloy. Unlike production Fulcrums, the structure was welded, not riveted. This saved weight because there was no need to seal rivet joints, and the new alloy had a lower specific gravity. The composite share was increased; besides the fins and various dielectric and access panels, composites were used for the airbrake, and inlet ducts. The use of

The first prototype MiG-29M, 151 Blue (the code-denoting item 15 No. 1), soars overhead during tests in Zhukovskiy. The stripe on the tailfin is part of the photo-theodolite target for attitude tracking. (Viktor Drushlyakov)

RAM reduced the aircraft's RCS by a factor of ten!

The pilot's seat was raised to improve visibility; this necessitated a canopy that was more convex than the Fulcrum-A/C's. The LERXes received a sharper leading edge to generate more powerful vortices at high alpha; this and the increased-span ailerons substantially improved the aircraft's low-speed handling. The stabilator area was increased by extending the leading edge and creating the characteristic dogtooth. Fin chord was increased below the rudders. The upper fuselage's contour was reshaped into a straight line. The APU air intake was relocated to starboard. The split airbrake of the standard MiG-29 was replaced by an Su-27 style, one-piece dorsal airbrake further forward. The landing gear was strengthened to absorb the higher gross weight.

The N-010 pulse-Doppler radar could track ten aerial targets while guiding AAMs to four priority threats. It was 60% lighter than the N-019. Outwardly, it could be recognized by a reprofiled radome with simple curvature. The helmet-mounted sight supplied target data to other targeting systems and IR-homing missiles. The aircraft could be fitted with a laser designator combined with a low-light-level TV or thermal imaging system. It had a completely new "glass cockpit" (EFIS) with an improved HUD, and two multi-function monochrome CRT displays for flight and target/weapons data; color CRTs could be integrated later on.

The ESM suite included a "Gardeniya-1FU" (L203B) active jammer and two BVP-60-26 chaff/flare dispensers with sixty 26-mm rounds each – twice the capacity of the Fulcrum-A. The dispensers were buried in the aft fuselage. The ECM aerials were ideally positioned at the wingtips under dielectric panels fore and aft, giving complete 360° coverage.

Six flying prototypes and a static test airframe were built. The first took to the air on April 25, 1986; it sported prominent T-shaped black-and-white phototheodolite calibration markings on the tail. It was powered by standard RD-33s because the uprated RD-33K had not yet completed its trials program. The second prototype was retrofitted with RD-33Ks in 1989. It was also the first to be fitted with the N-010 radar, a collimator HUD, and two CRT displays, thus becoming the first MiG-29M in representative production configuration. The aircraft was used for FBW testing, radar trials, handling, performance and field performance testing with and without external stores, and powerplant and fuel system testing.

The third aircraft was demonstrated at Kubinka AB on June 23, 1989. This, and the fourth and fifth prototypes, were used for engine, avionics, and systems testing, live air-to-air and air-to-ground firing trials, and cockpit ergonomics trials. The fourth aircraft in particular was used to verify the new IRST/LR, and the fifth prototype was for performance testing.

These port and starboard views of the fifth prototype, 155 Blue, were photographed in Akhtoobinsk. The recontoured fuselage spine and extended fin trailing edges are clearly visible. This aircraft was used primarily for performance testing. (Yefim Gordon archive)

The final prototype was built by MAPO in the early 1990s. The fifth and sixth aircraft were used for avionics trials (including electromagnetic compatibility trials) and live weapons firing trials against both aerial and ground targets, featuring a complete avionics suite with modifications introduced after the third prototype's tests.

Early test flights showed a marked improvement in maneuverability. The fighter had a maximum true airspeed (TAS) of 2,450 km/h (1,361 kts) or Mach 2.3, a maximum indicated airspeed (IAS) of 1,480 km/h (822 kts), and a 310 m/sec (1,017 ft/sec) rate of climb at 1,000 m (3,280 ft). Service ceiling was 17,000 m (55,774 ft), range on internal fuel 2,000-2,200 km (1,111-1,222 nm), and maximum ferry range with three drop-tanks 3,200 km (1,777 nm). With a 3,500 kg (7,716 lb) ordnance load, the aircraft had a 20-minute loiter time within 520 km (288 nm) from base. Combat radius was 1,250 km (694 nm) in dogfight mode (involving five 360° turns) with 2+2 short/medium-range AAMs and three drop-tanks.

The MiG-29M's G limits, rate of climb, and acceleration were roughly the same as in the production MiG-29/MiG-29UB. The maximum AOA, however, was much higher, enabling the fighter to make brief 9-G maneuvers with a full fuel load, which was

The top view illustrates the changes to the rear fuselage and the dogtooth on the stabilator leading edges characteristic of the MiG-29M. Note the false dorsal intake louvers, similar to production Fulcrums, added to confuse Westerners studying satellite imagery. (Yefim Gordon archive)

The MiG-29M shows off its characteristic ordnance load: Two Kh-29 AGMs, two Kh-31 AGMs, two R-73 AAMs, and two R-77 AAMs. Unusually, these are mounted asymmetrically in this photograph. (Yefim Gordon)

a major improvement over production aircraft. The MiG-29M had an electronic alpha limiter; initially the AOA limit was set at 30°, but this would be increased when the aircraft completed flight tests.

According to the development plan, the MiG-29M was to gradually supersede the Fulcrum-A/C on the MAPO production lines in the early 1990s. Within ten years the number of production MiG-29Ms would reach 300 or 400. Still, these hopes were shattered. The trials program was making slow progress; only the manufacturer's flight tests were completed by the early 1990s. These were deemed to be successful, even though both aircraft had to be grounded because of fatigue cracks. The state acceptance trials, however, were suspended because of funding shortages. The final flight under the state acceptance trials program was made in May 1993. Between them, the five prototypes made 1,068 flights.

According to MAPO-MiG estimates, the MiG-29M can match the performance of the Boeing/Lockheed F-22A Raptor fifth-generation fighter. Its combat potential is 1.5 times that of the Fulcrum-A/C in the counter-air role and 3.4 times better in the strike role.

MiG-29ME (MiG-33) Export Multi-Role Fighter

ANPK "MiG" are also working on a downgraded export version of the MiG-29M, designated MiG-29ME or MiG-33. This has a less capable WCS, which is borrowed from the MiG-29SD/SE based on the N-019ME radar.

MiG-29UBM Combat Trainer Project (*izdeliye* 9.61)

A trainer version of the MiG-29M, similar to the MiG-29UB, was under consideration for some time.

To stress the similarity and "generation change" from the MiG-29UB, the aircraft was designated MiG-29UBM. However, this remained a "paper airplane" because of the suspension of the MiG-29M program.

MiG-29Sh Attack Aircraft (Proposal)

After evaluating the MiG-29 in the strike role, MAPO-MiG proposed a specialized attack version of the

Fulcrum designated MiG-29Sh (*shtoormovik* – attack aircraft). The project was shelved due to lack of customer interest and funding.

MiG-29 (*izdeliye* 9.25) Multi-Role Fighter Project

Development work proceeded on this from the late 1980s; the main objectives were to extend range, improve agility, and integrate additional weapons.

These photos are from an air-to-air study of the fifth prototype MiG-29M, 155 Blue, and sixth prototype, 156 Blue. Both these aircraft were used for avionics trials and live weapons training against ground and airborne targets. (Aviatsiya i Kosmonavtika)

The new fighter was designated 9.25. It featured engines uprated to 10,000 kgp (22,045 lb st). The fuselage was stretched by moving the engines 910 mm (2 ft 11.82 in.) aft to make room for an additional integral fuel tank. Canard foreplanes were introduced and wing area was enlarged. A new WCS built around a new radar was fitted and the ordnance load was increased to 5,000 kg (11,023 lbs); the weapons range included anti-tank guided missiles.

The final change was the installation of new engines and a new avionics suite, which would turn the MiG-29 into a fifth-generation fighter. Fuel tank No. 2 was enlarged and a further tank (No. 5) was added, bringing the total to more than 8,000 lit. (1,760 Imp. gal.) – 40% more that the MiG-29M's and 90% more than the Fulcrum-A's. A refueling probe was also introduced. Initial VVS reactions were positive. Later, the program was shelved along with the MiG-29M as funding dried up.

The Kh-31P ARMs under the port wing are for air defense radar suppression, and the R-77 (RVV-AE) AAMs are used against aerial targets at medium range. 155 Blue was also used for cockpit ergonomics trials and extensive systems evaluation. (Viktor Drushlyakov)

The TV-guided Kh-29T missiles under the starboard wing are designed to destroy large-area ground targets while the R-73s are close-range "dogfighting missiles." (Yefim Gordon)

MiG-29 (*izdeliye* 9.35) Multi-Role Fighter Project

At a VPK MAPO press conference held on August 21, 1997, during the MAKS-97 air show, Mikoyan announced that an even more massive upgrade of the Fulcrum, referred to by the press as "MiG-35," was in the making. Since it had become clear by the late 1990s that no more money would be forthcoming for the MiG-29M, ANPK MiG decided to cheat the money from the stingy government by proposing an allegedly new-generation fighter. The fighter incorporated the improvements proposed for 9.25, albeit on a more modern technical level, and some ideas from the MFI program – the famous fifth-generation multi-role fighter known as Project 1.42.

It featured uprated engines with revised air intakes and inlet ducts, a 910-mm fuselage stretch, new radar, and an increased ordnance load. Internal fuel capacity was increased to approximately that of the MiG-29SMT. Besides the extra integral tank ahead of the engines and larger wing tanks, two strap-on fuselage tanks and integral tanks in the fin roots were added. It also had flight refueling capability. Because length and takeoff weight had grown, span and root chord was increased for wing area, and the result was quite similar to the MiG-25 Foxbat in planform, with lopped-off wingtips and a straight trailing edge.

This project seems to be suffering the same fate – the Russian MoD doesn't want it because it can't afford to buy it.

Trainer Derivative of *izdeliye* 9.35 (Proposal)

Concurrently with 9.35, ANPK MiG submitted a proposal for a two-seat trainer version. The aircraft dif-

fered mainly in having a new forward fuselage, retaining the improvements introduced on the single-seater. Unlike the MiG-29UB, the new trainer retained the fire-control radar. This was also put on hold.

MiG-29SMT Stage II Upgrade Project

Mikoyan proposed an upgrade of the MiG-29SMT. The so-called Stage II upgrade introduces RD-43 engines uprated to 10,000 kgp (22,045 lb st)

with thrust vectoring both in the pitch and the yaw plane. The (WCS) is built around an all-new "Zhemchoog" (Pearl) fire-control radar with a detection range of 130 km (72 nm) and 180° scanning in azimuth. The radar is capable of tracking ten targets at a time while guiding missiles to four priority threats.

The Stage II upgrade introduced a new BINS-SP navigation suite featuring ring laser gyros and correction via satellite link. The MiG-29SMT also featured a new "Kedr-29" (Cedar)

ESM suite comprising an RHAWS, active ECM, threat-distinguishing system and chaff/flare dispensers.

To guide advanced AGNs to their targets, the aircraft carries an IKSPOZ pod intended to expose targets. The MiG-29SMT Stage II can fill the tactical reconnaissance, interceptor, attack, and C[3] (command, control, and communications) roles. Experts estimate that it is eight times more effective than today's Fulcrum while being at least 35-40% cheaper to operate.

The landing of the same aircraft. Note the drogue chute pulling the tail chute from its housing between the mid-engine airbrakes. (Aviatsiya i Kosmonavtika)

MiG-29M 301 Blue (ex-156 Blue) sits at Mikoyan's flight-test facility in Zhukovskiy in April 1998. Note the absence of the fake dorsal intakes that suggested these were ordinary Fulcrum As or Cs. As this aircraft began to regularly visit the West, the deception was easily noticed. (Yefim Gordon)

Fulcrum-D, MiG-29K Shipboard Fighter (*izdeliye* 9.31)

Practical work to adapt fourth-generation fighters to CTOL carriers began on August 21, 1982, when the MiG-29KVP research aircraft made the first take-off from the provisional T-1 ski jump. Originally, it was intended that the MiG-29K would fill the counter-air role for the carrier group, and this drove the carrier design.

Full-scale development began in 1984. Two upgraded versions of the MiG-29 were being developed in parallel – the MiG-29M for the VVS and the MiG-29K for the AV-MF. The MiG-29K was to provide air defense for the carrier group day and night in any kind of weather at altitudes between 30,000 and 27,000 m (98,000-88,582 ft). Apart from air

defense, it was to act as a "hunter," destroying enemy ASW, transport, and AWACS aircraft; make anti-shipping strikes; support marine landings; escort land-based aircraft; achieve multiple kills; and perform reconnaissance tasks.

The MiG-29K's design was based on its land-based counterpart, the MiG-29M. Special attention was given to corrosion protection to enable operation in the salty ocean air. More stringent requirements applied to structural materials, coatings, seals, and gaskets. The fuselage (primarily the main fuel tank) was strengthened considerably to absorb the augmented loads during landings and arrested braking.

To reduce approach speed, wingspan was increased to 12.0 m (39 ft 4.44 in.) and wing area to 43 m² (462.36 sq. ft). The wings fea-

tured a modified TsAGI P-177M airfoil instead of the basic P-177, double-slotted flaps inboard, and flaperons outboard. The dorsal fin extensions housing the chaff/flare dispensers were removed, and the dispensers were incorporated in the aft fuselage. The outer wings folded hydraulically to a vertical position for hangar stowage, reducing span to 7.8 m (25 ft 7 in.). For better fatigue resistance, the wings were of welded-steel construction. The radome could be folded upwards to decrease overall length from 17.27 m (56 ft 7.92 in.) to 15.1 m (49 ft 6.48 in.).

The landing gear struts were lengthened, featuring heavy-duty increased-stroke shock absorbers and tiedown shackles. Special links shortened the struts during retraction to make sure they would fit into standard wheel wells. The nose-gear unit incorporated a modified steering mechanism, allowing the wheels to turn through ±90° for deck handling. It also had approach lights resembling a small traffic light to inform the landing signals officer (LSO) of the aircraft's position and speed on final approach. All wheels were fitted with new higher-pressure (285 psi) tires. The brake parachute was deleted; a quick-release FDR and the arrestor hook attachment and rebound damper were installed where the brake chute canister had been.

Removal of the dorsal auxiliary intakes made room for additional fuel in the LERXes, increasing the internal fuel capacity to 5,720 lit. (1,258.4 Imp. gal.) or 4,460 kg (9,832 lbs) of usable fuel. The total fuel load with three drop-tanks

Pre-production Aircraft 918 was fitted with an arrestor hook (the so-called "MiG-29KVP") during trials at the naval test centre, Saki AB. (stills from a Mikoyan video)

Aircraft 918 takes off from the ski jump at Saki. The ski jump was over 175 feet long and 18 feet high, with a 14.3 degree incline matching that of the proposed carrier. (stills from a Mikoyan video)

exceeded 6,500 kg (14,329 lbs). A fuel jettison system was provided to lighten the aircraft to the 15,300-kg (33,730-lb) maximum landing weight in the event of an emergency landing.

The MiG-29K was fitted with a fully retractable L-shaped refueling probe offset to port ahead of the windscreen; this allowed the fighter to receive fuel from any aircraft equipped with an UPAZ-1A-podded hose drum unit (HDU). For night refueling the probe was illuminated by a special retractable light. The arrestor hook was also illuminated during night landings.

The MiG-29K was equipped with an SN-K "Oozel" (Knot) navigation suite for overwater flights and carrier approach. It was more accurate and had a higher navigation data feed rate than previous systems. The MiG-29K had eight underwing weapons pylons and a centerline pylon. The ordnance load was increased to 4,500 kg (9,920 lbs) and included

A close-up of the arrestor hook mounted beneath the airbrakes on Aircraft 918. (Andrey Yurgenson)

311 Blue *was the first prototype MiG-29K shipboard fighter. The fuselage was strengthened to take the extra loads of arrested braking and no flare landings. (Mikoyan OKB archive)*

The first prototype MiG-29K makes a practice pass over SNS Tbilisi. Note the Kamov Search and Rescue helicopter in the background. (ITAR-TASS)

311 Blue *on SNS Tbilisi's deck with Toktar Aubakirov in the cockpit. Special corrosion protection was added to counter the effect of the salty sea air. (Yefim Gordon archive)*

eight combinations of AAMs and no fewer than 25 air-to-surface weapons options. Typical external stores in counter-air mode were four R-27s and four R-73s.

Specified combat radius was 850 km (472 nm) on internal fuel, increasing to 1,050 km (583 nm) with one drop-tank and 1,300 km (722 nm) with three. On-station time during combat air patrol (CAP) missions within 250 km (138 nm) from the carrier was 1.6-2.3 hrs. The crew escape system had a feature unique to the naval version: The ejection seat trajectory was inclined 30° sideways so that the seat would go overboard instead of falling on the deck.

Naturally, the structural changes added to the aircraft's empty weight. In normal takeoff configuration with four missiles and internal fuel only, the MiG-29K weighed 15,570 kg (34,325 lbs); MTOW with four missiles and three drop-tanks was 18,210 kg (40,145 lbs). The design took four years to accomplish. In early 1988 the factory began manufacturing two prototypes. The first completed its ground systems tests and flew for the first time in June. The trials program ended in 1991.

The aircraft was used at Novofyodorovka AB for extensive trials on the "unsinkable carrier" along with the MiG-29KVP testbed. By then the "Nitka" RDTC had been equipped with a representative S-2 arrestor

The MiG-29K makes its first carrier takeoff. The landing gear was both strengthened and lengthened with extra shackles to aid retraction. (Yefim Gordon archive)

We did it! The picture was taken immediately after the first deck landing. Note the arrestor wire on the tail hook. (Yefim Gordon archive)

"...into position and hold." Toktar Aubakirov aligns 311 Blue for takeoff. It is presumed that the nose-mounted frame was some form of primitive approach aid. (Yefim Gordon archive)

311 Blue, the first prototype MiG-29K, sits on the deck of RNS Admiral Kuznetsov (ex-Tbilisi) near the "rival" Su-27K prototype. These joint trials allowed a very honest comparison, operating in identical environments. (Yefim Gordon archive)

wire system and a "Luna-3" visual approach system. Seagoing trials commenced at the end of the month. Before a landing could be risked, however, a new series of test flights had begun on August 30; these quickly progressed into low passes over the carrier. On October 27 at about 11 A.M., the second prototype Su-27K appeared suddenly out of the mist to thunder over the flight deck.

Then the lighter MiG-29K prototype flew along the carrier's port side, judging the effect of the carrier's wake turbulence. Before making a real landing, Mikoyan, Sukhoi, and NII VVS pilots trained day after day, mastering the unfamiliar no-flare landing technique. The first conventional carrier landing in the Soviet Union was successfully accomplished at 1:46 P.M. by T10K-2. At 3:12 P.M. the MiG-29K followed suit, touching down somewhat more roughly; in fact, it appeared to onlookers that the aircraft dropped onto the deck like a gliding brick. Pictures of the first prototype aboard the carrier taken by a TASS reporter were circulated in November 1989, whereupon the MiG-29K received the NATO code name Fulcrum-D.

312 Blue was the second prototype MiG-29K shipboard fighter. The welded steel wings folded to reduce the span to 25 feet 7 inches. The nose radome folded upwards. (Yefim Gordon)

Some other views of the MiG-29K second prototype show that the nosewheel was modified to turn through 90 degrees to aid deck handling. (Yefim Gordon)

SNS *Tbilisi* completed her seagoing trials in 1991. On October 4 she was rechristened once again, becoming SNS *Admiral Kuznetsov*.

The second prototype, *312 Blue*, joined the flight-test program at its final stage. Besides flying, the final stage of the carrier's state acceptance trials included aerodynamic trials of the jet blast deflectors. The latter were a constant source of annoyance; not least because their water-cooling system had a propensity to explode when overheated, as demonstrated by the Su-27K on two occasions.

Thus the Fulcrum-D never got the chance to complete its state acceptance trials. There was another reason for this – a rather absurd accident. In the 13th flight of the state acceptance trials program, NII VVS test pilot V. M. Kandaoorov landed normally after a 1.5-hour sortie and inadvertently worked the landing gear control switch, selecting "gear up." Realizing his mistake, he immediately selected "gear down," but it was too late. The retraction jacks and hydraulic lines burst and the aircraft sank onto its belly, suffering serious damage. While *311 Blue* was undergoing repairs, the carrier departed for Novorossiysk – and that was it. Finito.

The first prototype made a total of 313 flights. Between them, Mikoyan and NII VVS test pilots made 74 carrier landings and a number of aerial refuelings. After the accident described above, *311 Blue* made another seven flights, bringing its total score to 320. The second prototype was grounded after only six flights. The uprated RD-33K engines behaved well throughout the trials program. The trials were suspended in early 1992. The Su-27K emerged as the winner, entering production in 1989 and becoming the Soviet Union's first operational CTOL shipboard fighter.

The MiG-29M was to gradually supersede the Fulcrum-A/C on the production lines in the early 1990s. Plans also included the pro-

312 Blue departing from Ghelendzhik airfield where it participated in the first hydro aviation show in September 1996. The antique Lisonuv Li-2 in the background unfortunately crashed near Moscow in 2004. (Yefim Gordon)

duction of 27 MiG-29Ks between 1986 and 1995. Defense spending cuts and the subsequent complete termination of state support for the program prevented the MiG-29K from reaching maturity. However, operational experience with the Flanker D and the *Admiral Kuznetsov*'s first Mediterranean cruise in December 1995 through March 1996 made the Russian Navy give some serious thought to reviving the MiG-29K program.

MiG-29KU Shipboard Trainer Project (*izdeliye* 9.62)

To facilitate conversion training, the Mikoyan OKB developed a projected two-seater version of the Fulcrum-D designated MiG-29KU (shipboard trainer). Only a full-scale mockup of the new forward fuselage was built, and this currently survives as a teaching aid at the Air Force Academy in Monino.

MiG-29SMT (*izdeliye* 9.17K) Shipboard Fighter Project

In late 1997, ANPK MiG proposed a navalised version of the MiG-29SMT to Russia's Ministry of Defence. The principal differences from the existing MiG-29K were increased range on internal fuel and a revamped cockpit with an EFIS identical to that of the MiG-29SMT. By February 1998 the project was still at the preliminary development stage. Mikoyan considered offering the aircraft to the Indian Navy. Alternatively, the aircraft could be purchased by the air force, and the STOL capability, beefed-up landing gear and arrestor hook could enable it to operate from short tactical airstrips equipped with ski jumps and arrestor systems.

The MiG-29K had its public debut in August 1992 when 312 Blue was in the static park at MosAeroShow '92 in Zhukovskiy. All the tires were increased to a higher pressure of 285 psi on the naval version. (Yefim Gordon)

In due time the Soviet Navy flag on the fins of the second prototype gave way to St. Andrew's flag of the Russian Navy. (Yefim Gordon)

MiG-29K 311 Blue is armed here with four Kh-31As and four R-77 (RVV-AE) medium-range AAMs. A tensioned wire helps support the folded wing tip while on display. (Yefim Gordon)

312 Blue *was present again at MAKS-2002 in Zhukovskiy. The tail hook replaced the drag chute between the airbrakes.*
(Yefim Gordon)

The nose part of the first MiG-29K prototype has every deck landing marked as a "kill" (near the photo theodolite marking). (Yefim Gordon)

A model of the proposed MiG-29KU shipboard trainer. Models of future projects give a great insight into the future thinking in Russian design bureaus. (Yefim Gordon)

INTO SERVICE

The MiG-29 achieved initial operational capability (IOC) several months before it was formally cleared for service. In July 1983 some 20 initial production aircraft were handed over with great ceremony to the 234th *Proskoorovskiy* GvIAP(fighter wing) based at Kubinka AB near Moscow. This unit, which can trace its history back to 1938, was traditionally the first to receive new types of fighters and was thus something of a "showcase unit."

The Fulcrum had first been demonstrated at Kubinka on April 7, 1981. Mikoyan test pilot Boris A. Orlov gave a brief 5-minute flying display to show what the new fighter could do.

"I engaged full burner," Orlov reminisced, "and the nearly 16 tons (35,273 lbs) of thrust pressed the air-craft's nose down. At a weight of 13 tons (28,660 lbs) the brakes could not hold the fighter and it crawled forward, tires squealing against the runway. I let go the brakes and the aircraft rushed forward like a dog which has burst its leash. The speed grew quickly ... NOW! I pulled back on the stick and the aircraft became airborne immediately. I continued hauling back to put it into a vertical climb as I retracted the gear. Now, climbing vertically at 400 km/h (222 kts), I checked the altitude – 1,200 m (3,937 ft), made a barrel roll, and put the nose down. At low altitude I checked my position and made a skewed loop, then a wingover, a turn, a three-quarters loop, putting the fighter into a vertical dive, then a half roll in the dive before pulling out. Finally, I passed over the runway, making a barrel roll over the middle of it, and broke to land."

The 4th Combat and Conversion Training Centre in Lipetsk was one of the first VVS units to receive the MiG-29. As early as the mid 1980s, the centre began developing operational recommendations and tactics for the type. The Centre's pilots performed mock combat between the MiG-29 and the production Su-27 (Flanker-B) to evaluate their respective merits and drawbacks. The pilots' opinion was that, despite the Su-27's FBW controls, pilot workload was greater than in the MiG-29.

By the end of 1991, MAPO's divisions at Moscow-Khodynka and in Lookhovitsy had built about 1,200 single-seat MiG-29s between them, and nearly 200 MiG-29UB trainers had been assembled in Gor'kiy. More and more VVS units were re-equipped with the new fighter as production increased.

By 1991 the VVS had some 800 Fulcrums on strength. They were operated by 25 fighter regiments, usually with 32 fighters to a unit (though some units had as many as 48 or 54 aircraft). Nearly 800 MiG-29s were permanently deployed abroad (in East Germany, Hungary, and Czechoslovakia). The biggest Fulcrum contingent was 250, stationed in East Germany with the Western Group of Forces. These included some very early-production aircraft with ventral fins, later supplemented with "fatback" Fulcrum-Cs.

Most aircraft wore standard two-tone grey camouflage. Some, however, had non-standard paint jobs. Many early Fulcrum-As had a very weathered finish which technical staff

MiG-29s at Kubinka AFB; those in the foreground are from the "Swifts" aerobatic team. (Yefim Gordon)

refreshed on site, painting up battered areas without worrying about an exact color match.

The MiG-29 was also stationed in other Warsaw Pact states, though in much smaller numbers. A single fighter division with 34 Fulcrums operated from airbases in Hungary. The 131st SAD included a fighter regiment operating 10 MiG-29s and 26 MiG-23s from Milovice AB in Czechoslovakia.

Ten MiG-29 regiments totalling some 350 aircraft were based in the European part of the Soviet Union. Two-thirds of these units were stationed outside Russia. The Ukraine had three units – in Mukachovo and Ivano-Frankovsk and at Martynovka AB. The last unit, part of the 5th VA (Odessa), operated a mixed bag of Fulcrum-Cs, MiG-29UBs, and MiG-23UBs. It was the only Fulcrum unit to be transferred to the Soviet Air Force's fighter-bomber arm.

In Belorussia, a fighter unit with 51 aircraft operated from Beryoza AB. Another unit with 35 Fulcrums was based at Tskhakaya AB in the Georgian Soviet Socialist Republic. This unit's name has come to be connected with a very unfortunate and widely publicized incident when one of its pilots defected to Turkey on May 20, 1989.

Capt. Aleksandr M. Zooyev was a first-class fighter pilot but a thoroughly rotten person; he was known as a "pocket Napoleon" – extremely vain and egotistical. Zooyev had been suspended from active duty some time before the incident because of poor discipline. Obviously, resentment at this coupled with his personality led him to commit treason. After sedating the pilots and ground crew of the quick reaction alert flight and

Anatoliy Kvochur, one of the world's best test pilots, is about to show the spectators what the Fulcrum can do, after a remarkably short takeoff. (Yefim Gordon archive)

The appearance of a single-seat MiG-29 and a two-seat MiG-29UB at the 1988 Farnborough International air show really made the headlines. It was one of the earliest public demonstrations that the Cold War was finally coming to an end. (Yefim Gordon archive)

An AV-MF fighter unit wearing the Soviet Navy flag operates this very early production MiG-29 (sans ventral fins). (Yefim Gordon archive)

cutting the telephone cables to prevent anyone from raising the alarm, he shot and seriously wounded a sentry on the ramp who tried to stop him. He then took off in one of the QRA MiG-29s despite also being wounded in the shootout. Subsequent analysis of FDR readouts showed that Zooyev had twice attempted to strafe the airfield before making for the border, but a safety feature of the internal gun foiled his plan.

The Turkish border was a mere ten-minute-flight from Tskhakaya AB. Another MiG-29 scrambled to intercept the defector but could not get within firing range before he entered Turkish airspace. Surface-to-air missile sites in the area were alerted but failed to detect the target because Zooyev was flying at ultra-low level to avoid radar detection. Thus Zooyev was able to cross the border unscathed, landing at the civil airport in Trabzon. The stolen fighter was returned the very next day pursuant to an agreement between the Soviet Union and Turkey. The defector's fate is unknown and despite insistent demands from the Soviet government, Zooyev was not extradited.

131 Fulcrums were based in the European part of the Russian Federation in 1990. Most of them were operated by training units and R&D establishments. No less than 79 MiG-29s resided at two instructional fighter regiments in Borisoglebsk. Fifteen Fulcrums were operated by the 234th

On June 8, 1989, 10 Blue crashed spectacularly at the Paris Air Show at Le Bourget during a demonstration flight on the opening day. Quick reaction and an excellent K-36D ejection seat saved Kvochur's life. (T.Shia)

SAP at Kubinka AB. The above units were part of the Moscow Defence District in the late 1980s.

Another MiG-29 unit with 40 aircraft operated from Orlovka AB in the Far East. Some Fulcrums were stationed in the Central Asian republics of the Soviet Union, including 22 aircraft in Turkmenia and 30 in Uzbekistan. There were also an unknown number in Kirghizia, where Loogovaya AB near the capital of Frunze served as a training centre for foreign MiG-29 pilots and ground crews.

Sqn 1 of the Combat Training Centre, located at Maryy AB, was the first VVS unit in Soviet Central Asia to master the Fulcrum. This was an "aggressor" unit, visitors often sporting sharksmouths and other gaudy nose art supposedly characteristic of the "potential adversary."

Originally, the unit's MiG-29s retained their factory finish and red tactical codes outlined in white. As

Company-owned MiG-29 999 White is a regular participant at air shows and is often demonstrated to foreign delegations. (RSK MiG/Arthur Sarkisyan)

The best company pilots are usually entrusted with performing demonstration flights. 506 Blue is seen here in a steep turn immediately before landing. (Yefim Gordon)

regular units operating the Fulcrum began visiting Maryy for a tussle with the "aggressors," however, telling the "good guys" from the "bad guys" became a problem, especially in air-to-air combat. The problem was solved by applying special markings to the upper surfaces of "aggressor" aircraft – known locally as "brandy stripes."

The Fulcrum was also operated by the AV-MF. In 1989 a complete fighter division comprising two MiG-29 regiments and a MiG-23 regiment was transferred to the Black Sea Fleet's air arm. One unit went at Limanskoye AB near Odessa and another at Markuleshty AB in Moldavia. In the early 1990s, one squadron of MiG-29s (12 aircraft)

was assigned to the Air Defence Command. The squadron was part of a fighter unit reporting to the 19th Independent PVO Army and operated from Privolzhskiy AB near Astrakhan' on the Volga river.

The political developments of the late 1980s in Eastern Europe and the subsequent collapse of the Soviet Union seriously affected the fate of MiG-29 units. On July 6, 1990, NATO's London summit passed a declaration on impending German reunification (October 3, 1990). Hence on September 12, a truly historic treaty was signed in Moscow under which the Soviet Union pledged to withdraw its troops from Germany.

The CIS leaders agreed that such units based in Belorussia (Belarus), Turkmenistan, Uzbekistan, and the Ukraine would remain there, becoming the basis of the air forces of these respective states. By early 1992 the Russian Air Force had some 300 MiG-29s on strength; more than half of them were still in Germany, awaiting redeployment to Russian airbases.

When the MAPO industrial association was formed, company demonstrators were adorned with the MAPO logo on the nose. (Yefim Gordon)

As on the Su-27, a typical ordnance load comprises two medium-range R-27 AAMs and four R-73 "dogfight missiles." (RSK MiG)

From its first days of MiG-29 operations, the 234th GvIAP started forming a display team flying the type. It was not until mid-1990, however, that the team was officially organized as the unit's Sqn 2 under the name Strizhi (Swifts). It was staffed with the unit's best Fulcrum pilots. The team had ten single-seat Fulcrum-As and three MiG-29UBs. All of them wore eye-catching colors with bright blue tails, blue/white wings, white engine nacelles, and a white fuselage with a black spine and blue lightning flash.

Originally, the Strizhi performed on four aircraft. Later, the team perfected the six-aircraft display technique in close formation, the aircraft flying within 3 m (10 ft) of each other. The Strizhi had their debut in France on May 13, 1991, performing at Reims-Champagne airbase.

Unfortunately, the MiG-29 has had its share of accidents. Forty-five Fulcrums have crashed as of April 1, 1998, with the loss of 23 pilots. The highest attrition rate was recorded in 1993 – 22 of the 31 VVS RF aircraft lost that year were MiG-29s. Only six crashes were caused by design and manufacturing defects. In 90% of the cases, pilot error was the cause of the accident. Staying on the ground certainly does not improve a pilot's flying skills!

The most famous accident was at the 38th Paris air show. On June 8, 1989, Mikoyan test pilot Anatoliy N. Kvochur was making a demo flight in *303 Blue*. During a high-alpha/low-speed pass at 160 m (525 ft) concluding the Fulcrum's aerobatics display, a flash of flame belched from the starboard engine's nozzle as the engine surged. Kvochur immediately selected full afterburner for the good engine, but at 180 km/h (100 kts) he had insufficient rudder and aileron authority to counter the asymmetric thrust.

Participants of the 1993 Royal International Air Tattoo (RIAT) at RAF Fairford saw a spectacular collision at 200-250 m (656-820 ft) in which one aircraft was virtually cut in two aft of the cockpit and burst into flames. Incredibly, both pilots escaped without a scratch, even though one of them had to eject inverted. In spite of these accidents,

This MiG-29 (izdeliye 9.13), with white "war game" recognition markings on the spine and fins, is operated by the Tactical Aviation Combat Training Centre (TsBP FA) in Lipetsk. (Yefim Gordon)

A curious formation, isn't it? Piloted by factory pilots, the two types built in Lookhovitsy – the MiG-29 and the Ilyushin Il-103 lightplane – make a low-speed flypast during the MAKS-97 air show in Zhukovskiy. (Yefim Gordon)

the MiG-29 has a far better safety record than many Western fighters. The Fulcrum is well liked by service pilots of the Russian Air Force.

The Western world got its first good look at the MiG-29 on July 1, 1986, when six Fulcrum-As from Kubinka AB visited Kuopio-Rissala AB in Finland. The MiG-29s lacked pylons so as to avoid revealing how many missiles the aircraft could carry.

Since there was no point in keeping the fighter veiled in secrecy anymore, the Soviet government made an unprecedented decision to demonstrate the MiG-29 at the 1988 SBAC air show at Farnborough. The appearance of two Soviet fighters created a veritable sensation. The Fulcrum quickly demonstrated its superiority to Western fighters present at the show. To quote Valeriy Ye. Menitskiy (then Mikoyan CTP), who was present at the show, "The joint practice sessions put everything into its proper place." The top of a loop executed on the MiG-29 is some 100 m (328 ft – Auth.) lower than on the F-16C or Rafale.

The MiG-29's tailslide maneuver performed by Kvochur and Taskayev was a true show-stopper, as it had been performed previously on competition aerobatic aircraft only, not on fast jets. First, it showed that the controls remained effective at ultra-low speeds (trajectory control was retained at zero and even negative airspeed when the aircraft briefly moved tail-first before exiting the maneuver in a dive). Second, it demonstrated the fighter's high thrust-to-weight ratio and smooth engine operation.

On April 26, 1995, Roman P. Taskayev set an altitude record in the 12-16 ton (26,455-35,273-lb) gross

Notice how neatly the nose gear retracts between the intakes on this single-seat MiG-29 of the Strizhi (Swifts) aerobatic team. (Yefim Gordon)

An attractive pattern is painted on the upper surfaces of the Strizhi aircraft, this time a UB. The colored wing pylons make an attractive detail. (Yefim Gordon)

weight class, climbing to 27,460 m (90,091 ft) in a standard MiG-29. In May the same year, a Fulcrum set another record, climbing to an altitude in excess of 25,000 m (82,020 ft) with a 1,000-kg (2,204-lb) payload. These records were officially recognized by the FAI at the year's end.

Apart from the Gulf War when Iraq made no real effort to oppose the Allies, the MiG-29 has never been in real combat. According to the USA, three Iraqi MiG-29s were shot down on January 17, 1991, and two more on January 19. The Iraqi pilots were definitely lacking in skill. German reunification gave NATO a chance to evaluate the MiG-29 in mock combat with the F-15 and F-16, which was especially welcome because Operation Desert Storm was already brewing at the time.

Mikoyan engineers believed in the Fulcrum, and their trust was rewarded. The MiG-29 has earned a good reputation for its reliability and maintainability. The aircraft is designed to be compatible with civil airfields meeting ICAO standards as well as with military bases. The fuel, power connectors, etc., are standardized, enabling the aircraft to use both Russian and Western ground support equipment. The connectors and access panels are conveniently located so that virtually all maintenance is done from ground level, with no need for stepladders.

The modular structure of the aircraft's systems, as well as a high degree of systems component interchange, eases maintenance and repair. Easy access to the engines facilitates engine maintenance and change. The built-in test equipment monitors more than 80% of the systems. The main problem facing the MiG-29's manufacturer and the Russian Air Force is not technical, but purely financial. Production of the Fulcrum virtually ground to a halt in 1991 because no funding was available.

Someone is making pre-flight checks on a MiG-29UB. The large, one-piece canopy greatly eases cockpit access. (Yefim Gordon)

The Strizhi in formation, extremely tight position keeping for such a large, swept-wing aircraft. (Yefim Gordon)

This MiG-29UB of the Strizhi team is doing solo aerobatics. The upper wing colors are matched on the undersides. (Yefim Gordon)

The traditional "fireworks" is displayed as each aircraft unleashes a salvo of IRCM flares at the end of the display. (Yefim Gordon)

OVERSEAS SALES

As of mid-1994, some 500 MiG-29s had been delivered to or ordered by the air forces of 16 nations. By 1997 the Fulcrum was in service in 23 states, including the CIS. Known operators of the type are dealt with in this chapter.

Belorussia

The Belorussian Republic had 47 aircraft on strength. Economic problems led them to put the Fulcrums up for sale. Eventually, Beltechexport signed a contract with the Peruvian government for the delivery of 18 MiG-29s to the Peruvian Air Force; the first four aircraft were shipped shortly afterwards. Some sources stated that the fighters were sold for US $11-14 million each. There have been rumors, however, that the price was closer to US $4.0-4.5 million each.

Bulgaria

In 1990 the Bulgarian Air Force took delivery of 12 MiG-29s – 10 single-seaters (9.12A) and 2 MiG-29UBs. Currently, Bulgaria is reported to have 21 or 22 on strength. Upgrades are now being undertaken at Graf-Ignatievo AB, the first Bulgarian base to be improved to NATO standards.

Cuba

Cuba was traditionally a Soviet ally and still enjoys "friendly nation" status. The Cuban Air Force received the state-of-the-art MiG-29 even before the collapse of the Soviet Union. The first aircraft arrived in October 1989 and made its checkout flight following reassembly on April

The fatback MiG-29 20 Yellow (ex-12) at Novofyodorovka AB in Saki is in very weathered current-style Ukrainian AF insignia. The aircraft is carrying two 1,150-lit. drop-tanks. (Viktor Drooshlyakov)

This Ukrainian Air Force MiG-29 (izdeliye 9.12) is one of 216 "claimed" by the country from the VVS and also CISAF stocks after they were withdrawn from Germany. (Yefim Gordon archive)

19,1990. There have been uncon-firmed reports that the FAR currently has one squadron of MiG-29s (twelve singles and two MiG-29UBs) on strength. The Fulcrums retain their two-tone grey factory finish.

Czech Republic

Czechoslovakia was one of the first socialist states to receive the MiG-29 (9.12A) and MiG-29UB. In 1988, fifteen carefully selected Czech Air Force pilots were sent to Loogovaya airbase near Frunze, the capital of the Kirghiz Soviet Socialist Republic, to undertake training. Deliveries began in the spring of 1989. The first aircraft arrived on April 24, 1989. Unlike most Ful-crums, Czech MiG-29s were painted in a so-called East European tactical camouflage (dark green/foliage green/dark earth/tan upper surfaces and light grey undersurfaces). The MiG-29s were used primarily in the air defense role. In 1991 CzAF pilots flew to Akhtoobinsk to train at the NII VVS firing range.

When the Federal Republic of Czechoslovakia split into the Czech Republic and Slovakia, the Fulcrum fleet was divided equally between the two. Having decided to join NATO, the Czech government was eager to dispose of Soviet equipment that did not conform to NATO standards and re-equipped the CzAF with western aircraft. Thus on December 22, 1995, a contract was signed with Poland and all ten Czech MiG-29s were trans-ferred to the Polish Air Force in exchange for new PZL Swidnik W-3 Sokól (Falcon) utility helicopters.

Germany

East Germany was the first of the Warsaw Pact countries to re-equip with the Fulcrum. Between March 1988 and May 1989, the East German

Ookrains'ki Sokoly (Ukrainian Falcons) MiG-29s (101 White and 109 White) take off from RAF Fairford for a six-ship display at the 1997 Royal International Air Tattoo. (Ryszard Jaxa-Malachowski)

Air Force received 20 MiG-29s (9.12A) and 4 MiG-29UBs. LSK/LV pilots had taken their conversion training in the Soviet Union in 1987.

East German Fulcrum-As also wore East European tactical camouflage and red serials. Conversely, the trainers had standard two-tone grey camouflage and, like all other LSK/LV aircraft, black serials.

When Germany reunited on October 3, 1990, the LSK/LV and the West German Air Force merged into a single *Luftwaffe*. There was much debate as to whether Soviet aircraft should be retained. Since the MiG-29 was the most modern of these, the German government decided to evaluate the type. To this end, two single-seaters and two trainers were transferred in late October to WTD 61 at Manching AB near Ingolstadt. The others remained at Preschen with JG 3.

The trials program comprised nearly 200 items. Performance, operational flexibility, and reliability of the weapons system as a whole and its various components were investigated. Operating and maintenance/overhaul costs were calculated. Equally important was how the MiG-29 would fare against NATO fighters in air-to-air combat. The latter came as a considerable shock as USAF F-15 and F-16 pilots often found themselves "shot down" in mock combat before they even got the Fulcrum on their radar screen!

Meanwhile, the German government addressed the Soviet Union, seeking aid in modifying the MiG-29s to make them compatible with NATO standards. The Soviet government authorized the Mikoyan OKB to do the job. The *Luftwaffe* proposed that Mikoyan check and authorise all the changes, and so they did. The fighters were fitted with new identification friend-or-foe (IFF), communications and tactical navigation (TACAN) equipment, flight instruments marked in feet and knots, an "English-speaking" version of the "Ekran" (Screen) ground test system, anti-collision strobe lights, etc. Even the colors of the artificial horizon changed to suit NATO requirements. The instruments were altered in Moscow and delivered to Germany for installation; the rest of the changes were made on-site.

Post-modification trials were held in April and May 1991 in Italy at the Air Combat Maneuvering Installation (ACMI) at Decimomannu AB, Sardinia. The Fulcrums won in all

The Ookrains'ki Sokoly show off their patriotic color scheme during a practice session. (via Viktor Markovskiy)

With the exception of a single MiG-29UB trainer, all Moldovan MiG-29s acquired by the USAF wore a crudely applied non-standard green camouflage. Not all had the gaudy Moldovan insignia, as illustrated by these Fulcrum-Cs. Note the access hatches to the avionics bays. (AFM)

sessions of mock combat against various NATO fighters. Thus the Fulcrum gained the distinction of being the only Soviet type to remain with the *Luftwaffe* after reunification.

Hungary

The Hungarian Air Force had 22 singles (9.12B) and 6 MiG-29UB trainers delivered by Russia as foreign debt payment. They are operated by the 9th fighter regiment at Kecskemet.

India

The Indian Air Force (IAF) was the first foreign operator of the MiG-29. India approached the Soviet government in the early 1980s, requesting the delivery of the latest Soviet fighters. This was because F-16s were delivered to the Pakistani Air Force, potentially disrupting the regional balance of power. When the Soviet Minister of Defence visited India in February 1984, he agreed that the Soviet Union would supply India with 44 MiG-29s (40 Fulcrum-As and 4 Fulcrum-Bs) at US $11 million each. License production of a further 110 aircraft was also discussed.

Indian MiG-29 pilots were trained at Loogovaya AB. In December 1986 the first 12 aircraft were delivered in

The MiG-29UB 61 White is being loaded into a USAF C-17A at Markuleshty. This was one of a batch taken out of circulation by the USA under the Co-operative Threat Reduction Program. (AFM)

The single ex-Moldovan MiG-29UB acquired by the USAF (61 White) wore an unusual dark blue/pale blue color scheme, suggesting it was used for display purposes. (AFM)

This Czech AF MiG-29 is marked with a "tiger" stripe signifying the squadron's participation in European "Tiger Meets." (Helmut Walther)

One of the Cuban single-seat aircraft, 911, taxis at San Antonio de los Banos. The Cubans received the MiG-29 before the collapse of the Soviet Union, but they are rarely seen or photographed. (World Air Power Journal)

the form of semi-knocked-down (SKD) kits to HAL's Nasik factory. The official handover ceremony took place at Poona AB on December 6, 1987.

By early 1997 the IAF had taken delivery of 72 single-seat MiG-29s (9.12B standard) and 8 MiG-29UBs. (There have been allegations, however, that India refused to accept the down-graded export version and managed to persuade the Soviet Union to deliver the fully capable 9.12). The aircraft were delivered in standard Soviet two-tone grey camouflage. Later, some IAF Fulcrums got some non-standard paint jobs with highly colorful tails for participation in war games.

Still wearing full Czech AF insignia and 11.SLP tiger stripes, five MiG-29s newly acquired by the Polish AF are seen at Minsk-Mazowiecki immediately on arrival. (Ryszard Jaxa-Malachowski)

East German Air Force MiG-29s wore three-digit red serials on the air intakes. Originally operated from Preschen, they later moved to Laage on the northern coast before being sold to Poland in 2004. (Martin Baumann)

Indian pilots praised the MiG-29, especially the ten aircraft of an unspecified new version delivered in 1995 (some sources say 1996). These aircraft had increased airframe and engine life, improved armament, and upgraded fire-control radars that could track ten targets at a time while guiding missiles to two priority threats. The IAF is now considering upgrading the earlier aircraft to this standard. The MiG-29 was known locally as the Baaz (Eagle).

Iran

After the war with Iraq ended in 1988, Iran decided to follow the example of its warlike neighbor and order the MiG-29. The aircraft were declared operational on October 7, 1990. The exact quantity is unknown; there have been unconfirmed reports that the IRIAF operates 14 MiG-29s (9.12B), but MAPO-MiG stated unofficially that several dozen were delivered in all. Iran retained nine ex-Iraqi MiG-29s flown to Iran during the first Gulf War.

Iraq

Iraq was the second Middle Eastern state to express an interest in the MiG-29, ordering 48 of the type in 1987. The first 18 aircraft (9.12B standard and some MiG-29UBs) were delivered late the same year. Iraqi Air Force Fulcrums were used in the air defense role, operating mostly from bases around Baghdad.

No reliable information as to how many MiG-29s were actually operated by the Iraqi Air Force is available. Unconfirmed reports state that 35 Fulcrum-As and 6 Fulcrum-Bs were on strength in August 1990. The first 18 aircraft reportedly wore desert camouflage; the rest were delivered in standard Soviet two-tone grey camouflage.

Iraqi Fulcrums were just about the only ones to fire in anger, being used operationally in the Gulf War that followed Iraq's invasion of Kuwait on August 2, 1990. At least eight were reported shot down in dogfights by USAF F-15s and US Navy F/A-18s during Operation Desert Storm that began in February 1991. Nine MiG-29s, along with many other Iraqi Air Force aircraft, were flown to neighboring Iran for safety. There the aircraft and pilots were interned, and the Fulcrums were retained by Iran as reparations for damage done during the Iran-Iraq war.

MiG-29 29+17 and 29+05 in Luftwaffe's current light grey air superiority color scheme. As with most Fulcrums, the wheel hubs tend to stay in the military green, whatever the overall colors. (Marcus Fulber)

A Luftwaffe MiG-29 on display at ILA 2004. Note the gun port in the port wing root. (Yefim Gordon)

Israel

Western information agencies reported that several MiG-29s landed at Sedom airbase in the Negev Desert in southern Israel sometime in 1997. Their origin is unknown, nor is there any information as to whether the aircraft had actually been sold to Israel or simply leased for evaluation purposes.

There have also been unconfirmed reports that in 1990 Israel took possession of a Syrian Air Force MiG-29 whose pilot defected.

29+23, one of the Luftwaffe's four MiG-29UBs, is seen here taxiing with louvers open. (Henrik Glienke)

Kazakhstan (Kazakstan)

Kazakhstan – or Kazakstan, as this CIS republic has been called of late – has taken over a few ex-VVS MiG-29s based there. Unfortunately, the number operated is unknown.

Malaysia

On June 7, 1994, Russia and Malaysia signed a US $560 million contract for the delivery of 16 single-seat MiG-29s and 2 MiG-29UB trainers to the Royal Malaysian Air Force. The contract stated that the aircraft were to be delivered with a higher gross weight (increased ordnance load) and more capable avionics, including radar. After delivery the singles were to be retrofitted with refueling probes.

The Malaysian Fulcrums were not purpose-built under the contract; these fighters, manufactured in 1988-1990 (mostly Batch 52 aircraft) had been languishing at the factory airfield in *Continued on page 73*

Tired Hungarian MiG-29 pilots discuss a sortie after returning to Kecskemet Air Base south of Budapest. (Yefim Gordon archive)

This East German Air Force MiG-29UB, 179, was delivered in April 1988 and went on to be 29+23 in unified service. (Flieger Revue)

COLOR SECTION/DRAWINGS

This Fulcrum C single-seat MiG-29 with the trainer Fulcrum B is clearly showing the landing gear retraction process and wing and tail control surfaces.

506 Blue, *a company demonstrator, is seen here bearing the unusual three-figure fin code and carrying four R-73 dogfighting missiles and two R-27R medium-range radar homing AAMs. Note the engine intake louvers.*

A ground shot of 150 Blue *clearly shows the position of the nose-gear scraper-type mud/slush/snow guard for FOD protection. This is essential for unprepared landing strips and poor weather operations.*

With full reheat selected on take-off, the MiG-29 has an impressive rate of climb of over 1,000 feet per second. Note the brake parachute container nestling between the rear ventral and dorsal airbrakes.

This underside view of 150 Blue, a MiG-29 Fulcrum-A (izdeliye 9.12), shows the well-defined separation of the twin engines. Seen here in "clean" configuration with four under-wing hardpoints, one can appreciate the elegant design of the airframe.

MiG-29 (izdeliye 9-13) 05 Red is on a test flight from the Akhtoobinsk test airfield, showing the wing-mounted bomb racks. These can carry 100-kg or 250-kg bombs. The intake louvers may be opened during low-speed flight.

MiG-29 (izdeliye 9-13) 05 Red on a test flight from the Akhtoobinsk test airfield, shows the bomb racks from the front. Note the offset IRST unit forward of the cockpit, which allows highly accurate target finding without the radar. This enables the pilot to fire an accurate first cannon burst, thereby preserving limited ammunition.

This special-marks Luftwaffe MiG-29 is staying with the unified German forces after the collapse of East Germany. These Fulcrums were transferred to Poland in mid-2004.

Another special-marks Luftwaffe MiG-29 is painted to celebrate the end of active service with German forces in 2003. It appeared at various European events prior to transfer to the Polish Air Force.

The first prototype of the ship-borne variant MiG-29K featured folding wings and normally carried anti-shipping missiles, typically Kh-31As, as well as air-to-air weaponry. Note the deployed refueling probe fitted to port. The harsh Soviet winter demanded a truly all-weather capability.

The rear-view mirror, HUD, and ejector seat are clearly visible in the relatively spacious cockpit of this MiG-29. The test pilot is clearly satisfied with his working environment.

The MiG-29M2 falls back from a tail-slide, revealing the intense reheat at the core of its RD-33K engines. Wing-mounted smoke generators have been fitted for public performances.

The MiG-29M2 makes a vertical climb just before performing its famous tail-slide at a summer air show. The tail slide demonstrated the fighter's high thrust-to-weight ratio and smooth engine operation throughout its flight envelope. Note the new "dogtooth" leading edge on the stabilators.

Vladimir Gorbunov, "Hero of Russia," made the first flight of the MiG-29SMT on April 22, 1998. He succeeded Roman P. Taskayev as Mikoyan chief test pilot in the fall of 1997. Note the ease of entry into the large cockpit, as well as the twin rear-view mirrors on the canopy frame.

This line of active Fulcrums is in frontline service. The contrast between the high-tech fighters and their typically Soviet-style support vehicles says much about military infrastructure.

The second prototype MiG-29SMT, 917 Blue, is seen here at Zhukovskiy. The large weapons on the inner wing pylons are Kh-31P anti-radiation missiles. The formidable array of weaponry has effectively upgraded the SMT to a "generation 4+" fighter. Note the 1,500-liter centerline drop-tank.

Unlike the MiG-29UB, the UBT combat trainer has full weapons capability. The rototype, 304 Blue, is seen here at Zhukovskiy. The front cockpit is virtually identical to that of the SMT, and the rear features three large LCDs. It first flew on August 25, 1998, and appeared at Farnborough, England, nine days later.

Two MiG-29UBTs of the Strizhi (Swifts) aerobatic team on take-off. Formally formed in 1990 as squadron 2 of the 234th GvIAP with 10 Fulcrum-As and three Ubs, their international reputation began at Reims, France, in 1991. The original blue colors have now given way to this striking red, white, and blue livery.

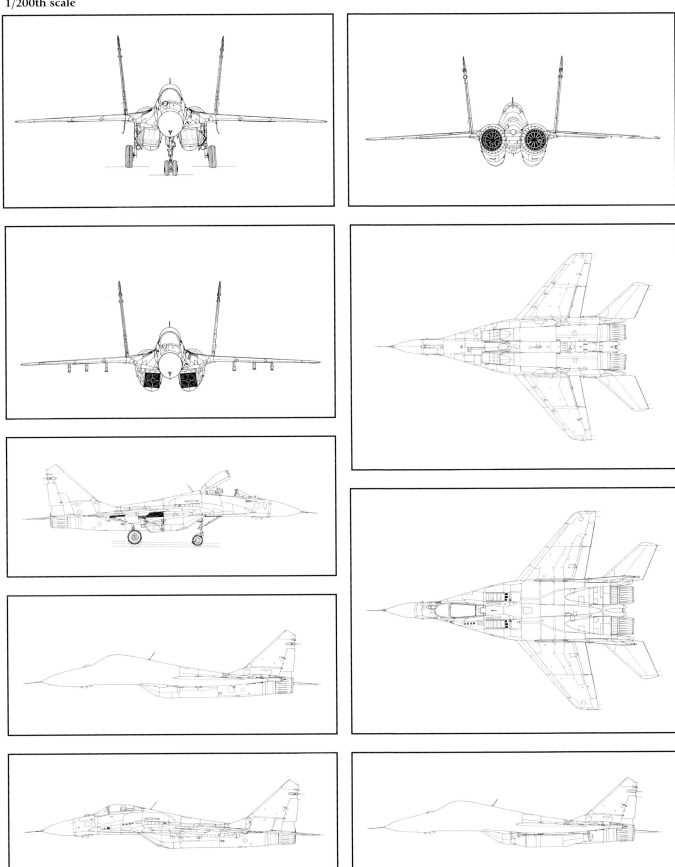

Nine views of production MiG-29 Fulcrum-A (izdeliye 9.12).

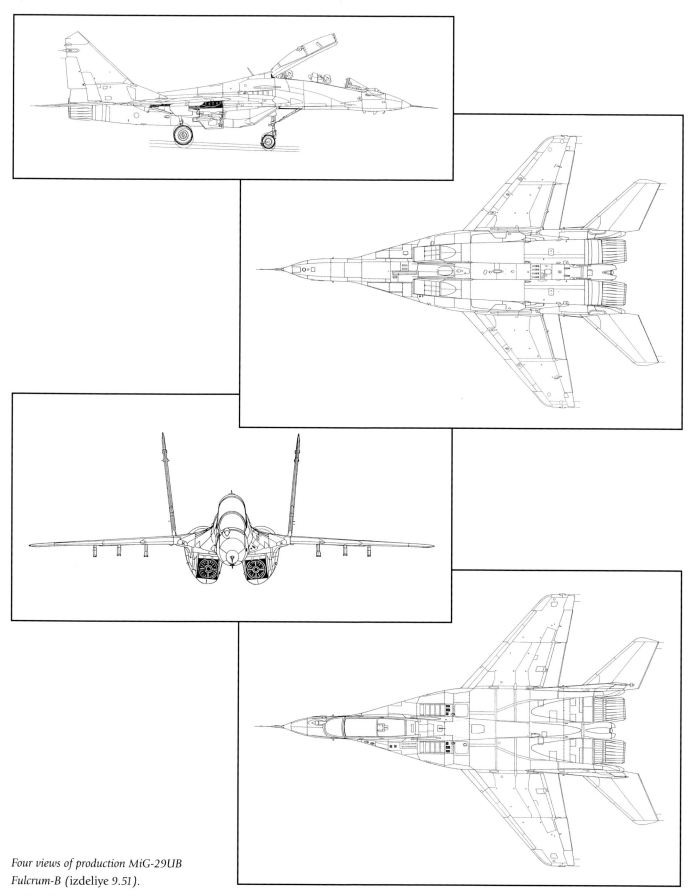

*Four views of production MiG-29UB
Fulcrum-B (izdeliye 9.51).*

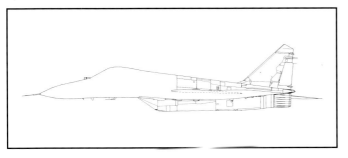

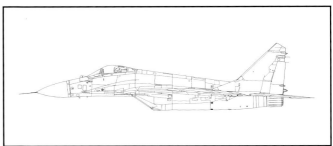

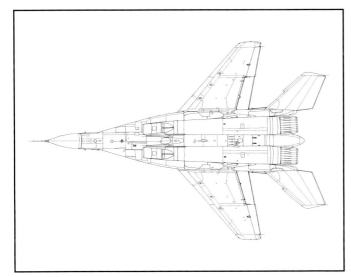

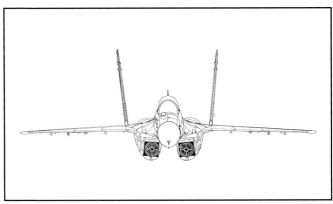

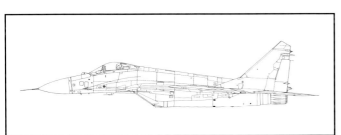

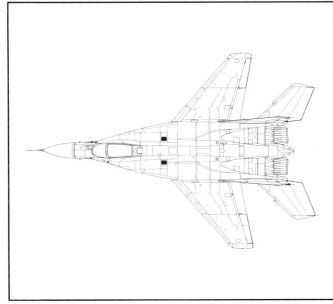

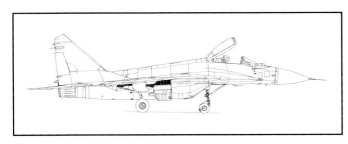

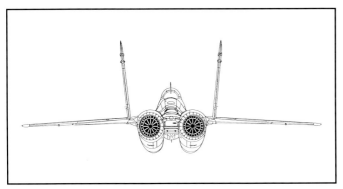

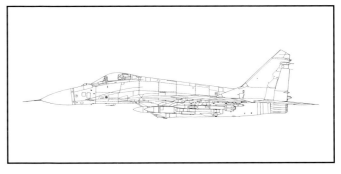

Nine views of MiG-29M prototypes (izdeliye 9.15, Blue 151, 155, and 156).

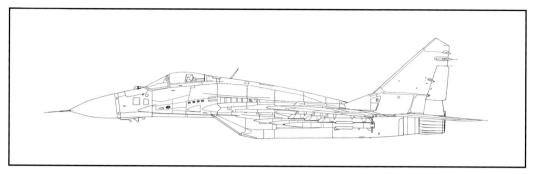

MiG-29S
(izdeliye 9.13, 407 Blue)

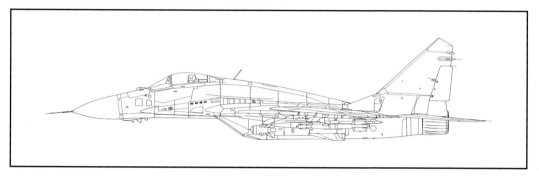

MiG-29SM

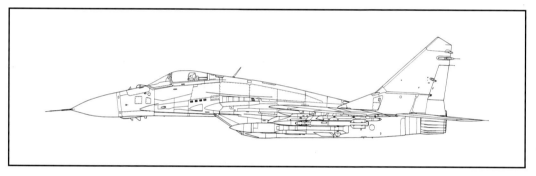

MiG-29SMT
(izdeliye 9.17)

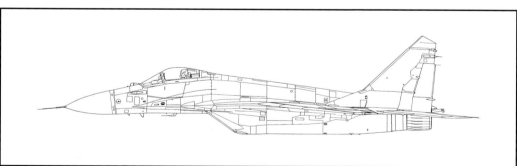

MiG-29K (izdeliye 9.31)

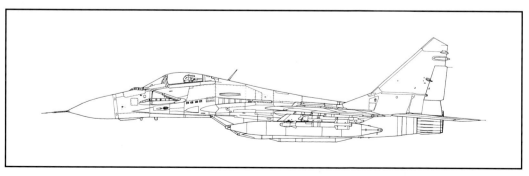

MiG-29 refueling system
testbed (357 Blue)

Lookhovitsy, unclaimed, and unpaid for, by the Soviet (and since Russian) Air Force.

In the spring of 1996 the MiG-29s participated in a TUDM exercise, earning high praise from military experts. On April 12-30, 1997, the Flying Fish '97 exercise was staged in the South China Sea by the forces of the UK, Australia, New Zealand, and Malaysia. Observers at the exercise were particularly impressed by the MiG-29's performance.

Moldova

After the collapse of the Soviet Union, a good deal of military equipment was left behind in the now-independent CIS states. Moldova inherited a MiG-29 unit. The 31 (or 33) aircraft included 7 very early aircraft with ventral fins and at least 1 MiG-29UB.

The Republic was just too small for the MiG-29s, however, and there was always the danger of intruding inadvertently into foreign airspace. Four aircraft were sold to South Yemen. But Yemen soon dropped

India was the first-ever foreign operator of the MiG-29. Delivery was requested to balance F-16s ordered by neighboring Pakistan. (Simon Watson)

This rare photo shows an Islamic Iranian Air Force MiG-29 displayed at Mehrabad International Airport. (AFM)

In May 1987 two IAF fighter squadrons – 47 Sqn "Archers" and 28 Sqn "First Supersonics" – were re-equipped with MiG-29s assembled at the HAL factory in Nasik. (World Air Power Journal)

Moldova as an arms supplier because the aircraft came incomplete and without adequate technical support.

On September 6, 1997, Russian media announced that the USA had bought 21 ex-Moldovan Fulcrums – 6 Fulcrum-As, 14 Fulcrum-Cs, and a single MiG-29UB. The reason for this deal is noteworthy. Moldova kept looking for customers and, among other countries, approached Iran which already operated the type. This was the least desirable customer as far as the USA was concerned. The Fulcrum-C has tactical nuclear strike capability, which is why the USA offered to buy the Fulcrums wholesale in order to prevent them from going to "rogue states." There have been unconfirmed reports that the deal was worth US $80 million. If this is true, Moldova sold the fighters dirt-cheap – at about US $4 million apiece. All the aircraft were sold in semi-dismantled condition ready for shipment.

North Korea (Korean People's Democratic Republic)

North Korea became the second Asian state to order the MiG-29. The type was purchased in response to the threat posed by South Korea's new F-16C/Ds. North Korea is unique among foreign MiG-29 operators in two respects. First, it is the only country to have purchased manufacturing rights, and second, it is the only country outside the Soviet Union/CIS to operate five or six Fulcrum-Cs. These were delivered as SKD kits and assembled on-site. Unlike Soviet Air Force Fulcrum-Cs, the North Korean aircraft do not have the L203B "Gardeniya-1FU" active jammer.

The first fighters were assembled in May-June 1988, and delivery of the entire order was completed by the end of the year. (Some sources state that the initial batch contained 12 aircraft and the total did not exceed 20.)

Peru

After losing in a border conflict with Ecuador in 1996, Peru decided to order MiG-29 fighters. Initially the Peruvian government approached Russia on this subject, but then the Peruvian Air Force unexpectedly bought 16 ex-Belorussian Fulcrums – 14 single-seaters and 2 MiG-29UBs – together with a load of R-27, R-60, and R-73 AAMs; 80-mm S-8 unguided rockets; incendiary bombs; and support equipment. The FAP officially accepted the fighters at Las Palmas AB near Lima on July 29, 1997.

Belorussia, however, was unable to supply spares and ammunition, provide maintenance, etc., and Russia had warned in advance that it would not service aircraft sold by third parties. Only four of the FAP's MiG-29s remained operational in the autumn of 1997.

Poland

The Polish Air Force ordered 12 Fulcrums, and deliveries began in 1989 after a group of PWL pilots took their training in the Soviet Union the preceding year. The first four MiG-29s (9.12A) arrived at Minsk-Mazowiecki airbase early that summer. They were followed by three MiG-29UBs on August 1, 1989, and five more Fulcrum-As on October 30, 1990.

This Iraqi MiG-29 (izdeliye 9.12B) is apparently at some form of military exhibition. (World Air Power Journal)

FAP 045, one of the Peruvian Air Force MiG-29Ubs, was delivered in 1997 and operated by 6 group based near Lima. (AFM)

After the dissolution of the Warsaw Pact, Poland began pushing for NATO membership. This involved switching to NATO standards, so Poland decided not to buy Russian equipment anymore, including aircraft. Yet economics outweigh politics, and the Czech decision to phase out the MiG-29 came as a real (and probably unexpected) gift to the PWL. The 10 CzAF aircraft were traded profitably for W-3 Sokól helicopters, bringing the total in PWL service to 22, and the Polish government was quite happy to strike the deal.

Romania

In 1989 a group of Romanian Air Force pilots completed their conversion training at the Kiev Air Force Academy. In November-December they ferried their new mounts – ten MiG-29s (9.12A) and two MiG-29UBs – to Constanta. Later deliveries brought the total up to about 30 aircraft. According to ANPK MiG, Romania later purchased a single MiG-29 from neighboring Moldova, quite possibly as an attrition

replacement. Many of these are now in storage.

Slovakia

Unlike the Czech Republic, Slovakia still regarded Russia as a prime trade partner and military ally. Therefore, the Slovakian air arm retained the nine Fulcrum-As and single Fulcrum-B received after the division of Czechoslovakia.

In early 1994 Slovakia took delivery of five MiG-29s of an unspecified new version and a single MiG-29UB. Eight more Fulcrum-As were supplied later, bringing the total to 24.

South Yemen (People's Democratic Republic of Yemen)

In mid 1993 Moldova sold four or five of its MiG-29s to the South Yemen Air Force via a third party. However, it turned out that the aircraft were delivered incomplete and two were in non-airworthy condition. The others were soon grounded.

Poland was one of the first Warsaw Pact countries to take delivery of the MiG-29, the first of 12 being delivered in 1989. They are based at Minsk-Mazowieki to the east of Warsaw. (Waclaw Holys)

The MiG-29 is Poland's most modern fighter. The Polish AF constantly keeps several Fulcrums on Quick Reaction Alert (QRA). (Waclaw Holys)

Syria

The Syrian Arab Republic was the second export customer for the MiG-29. This Middle East country traditionally operated Soviet military hardware and needed new fighters to replace aircraft lost in wars with Israel.

Syria ordered 150 Fulcrums in April 1987. Deliveries commenced quickly; the first aircraft – single-seat MiG-29s (9.12B) and two-seat MiG-29UBs – were handed over to the Syrian Air Force in July. The first MiG-29 squadron became operational in October 1988. A second batch was delivered by the end of the year, bringing the total strength to one regiment (three squadrons).

Slovak Air Force MiG-29 7501 is in a special display color scheme. (Peter Davison)

*The former Yugoslavia was the first European country to operate the MiG-29, 14 singles and 2 trainers being delivered by early 1988. (*World Air Power Journal*)*

There have been no confirmed reports of Syrian Fulcrums in action against Israeli jets. Rumor has it that a Syrian pilot defected to Israel in a MiG-29, but again this has not been officially confirmed. What *is* known, however, is that the Syrian Air Force never got the 150 MiG-29s originally ordered. It is generally believed that deliveries stopped at 80; however, the latest reports from ANPK MiG and other sources state that only 20 were delivered.

There were unconfirmed reports originating from Israeli sources that a Syrian MiG-29 pilot defected to Israel in 1990 and that at least one more MiG-29 was lost in a shootout with IDF/AF fighters in early 1991.

Turkmenistan

Turkmenistan's small air arm includes 12 to 40 ex-VVS Fulcrum-Cs (9.13 or 9.13S); it is not known if other versions are operated.

The Ukraine

After the breakup of the Soviet Union, the Ukrainian Air Force (UAF) took possession of all ex-VVS aircraft based in the republic, as well as some of the CISAF aircraft being withdrawn from reunified Germany. These included 216 MiG-29s, including 155 Fulcrum-Cs (9.13 and 9.13S). Thus, the Ukraine is the world's second-largest MiG-29 operator.

In the early 1990s the UAF got its own display team, the "Ookrains'-ki Sokoly" (Ukrainian Falcons). The team operates five single-seat Fulcrum-As and two MiG-29UB trainers.

Once again, because of economic difficulties and the inability to keep large armed forces, the Ukrainian government has been trying to sell off part of its military aircraft, including some of the MiG-29s. Sales prospects, however, have been ham-

The Malaysian Air Force (TUDM) was pleased with the Fulcrum. The type has performed exceptionally well during military exercises. (Yefim Gordon archive)

pered by the inability to provide spares (as these have to be sourced in Russia) and adequate maintenance.

United States of America

The US Air Force got its first chance to evaluate the MiG-29 when one of the *Luftwaffe*'s Fulcrum-As was loaned to the Air Force Systems Command (AFSC) in 1990. The objectives included development of anti-MiG-29 tactics and countermeasures for the impending Operation Desert Storm, during which USAF and USN fighters expected to be opposed by the Fulcrum. The aircraft remained in the USA at least until August 1992.

In late 1997, as mentioned earlier, the USAF bought 21 ex-Moldovan MiG-29s – 6 Fulcrum-As, 14 Fulcrum-Cs, and a single MiG-29UB. The deal was part of the Co-operative Threat Reduction Program initiated in 1993. The aircraft were bought in dismantled condition and delivered to Wright-Patterson AFB, Ohio.

Uzbekistan

After the collapse of the Soviet Union, Uzbekistan took over 36 "fatback" MiG-29s (9.13 or 9.13S);

This Malaysian MiG-29N is being loaded for delivery into a Russian AF Antonov An-124 Ruslan freighter. (Viktor Drushlyakov)

the exact quantity is unknown. It is not known if other versions are operated.

Yugoslavia/Serbia

Yugoslavia became the first European export customer for the Fulcrum in 1987. By early 1988 the Yugoslav Air Force had taken delivery of 14 9.12As and two MiG-29UB trainers. They were operated by the 127th LAE at Batajnica airbase. An immediate problem arose when the Fulcrums arrived – they were too big to fit into the underground

hardened aircraft shelters (HAS) built for the MiG-21s they supplemented, so new shelters had to be built.

Yugoslavia traditionally allocated indigenous designations to new types included in the JRV inventory; thus, the MiG-29 became L-18. Another 16 aircraft were due for delivery in 1988, but no additional MiG-29s were supplied before the Serbo-Croat civil war broke out and all weapons sales were embargoed. After the breakup of Yugoslavia into five separate states, the fighters were retained by the Serbian Air Force.

THE MiG-29 COMPARED

More than 500 Fulcrums had been delivered to, or ordered by, 16 nations by mid-1994, making it the F-16's most serious competitor on the world fighter market.

The MiG-29 was a light fighter, continuing the MiG-15/17/21 philosophy. Like its predecessors, it was required to have high speed, rate of climb, and service ceiling, because high-flying spy planes were among its main targets. Obtaining good field performance (without resorting to VG), low-speed handling, and all-round visibility were priorities. The aircraft was required to have maximum engine power and low-wing loading.

Briefly, the F-16 and the MiG-29 compare as follows. The F-16 is an air superiority fighter designed to operate together with the heavier F-15. Conversely, the MiG-29 was to gain air superiority in the forward battle area *without* working in concert with the heavier Su-27 Flanker. Thus, the Fulcrum fits into a niche between the F-16 and the F-15 as regards armament and equipment but has shorter range.

Both the F-16 and the MiG-29 are stressed for nine Gs. Both aircraft have prominent LERXes and air intakes suited to high-alpha operation. The MiG-29 uses an integral layout in which the wings and fuselage are blended into a single lifting body. The F-16 is designed along more conventional lines with a classic separate fuselage. Since the Fighting Falcon was optimized for maximum maneuverability at transonic speeds, a fixed-area monoshock air intake was chosen. This enabled the engine to run steadily at up to Mach 2.0.

The MiG-29 was designed for higher speeds, so Mikoyan engineers opted for variable four-shock intakes enabling steady engine operation at up to Mach 2.3. In both cases, the intakes were located ventrally to minimize airflow distortion at high alpha or during tight turns. For the same reason, General Dynamics made the inlet duct as short as possible, but it was limited by the nose-gear unit stowed beneath the inlet duct. Mikoyan achieved the same result by placing the intakes under the LERXes that directed the airflow.

The different air intake design was also explained by the different approach to the FOD prevention problem. US specialists believed the F-16's air intake design made foreign object ingestion unlikely, since the intake was located forward of the nose gear. Soviet airfields were usually in much worse condition, hence the increased risk

Another important difference is the tail unit design. General Dynamics had considered both single and twin vertical tails for the F-16 at the PD stage. Wind tunnel tests showed that the vortices generated by the LERXes maintained their direction at high AOAs, and twin tails gave slightly better directional stability. Eventually, however, a single fin and rudder was chosen. Mikoyan opted for twin tails because the MiG-29 was designed for higher speeds and more stringent requirements applied to directional stability; besides, the twin-tail layout had been tried and tested on the MiG-25 Foxbat. The tail unit worked with four vortices generated by the LERXes and vortex generators on the pitot boom.

The F-16 has trapezoidal wings (almost a cropped delta) with a 40° leading-edge sweep, an aspect ratio of 3.2, and a 4% thickness-to-chord ratio at the roots. The MiG-29's wings have similar LE sweep (42°) and a marginally higher aspect ratio (3.5); theoretically this should result in slightly higher drag.

The F-16 is the world's first production fighter to feature an FBW control system. In contrast, the MiG-29 has conventional mechanical controls. The advanced MiG-29M, however, does incorporate FBW controls that enhance its combat capabilities.

Despite the MiG-29's good high-alpha handling, the pilots cannot fully use it to shorten the landing run since the landing gear is fairly short. Touching down at 240 km/h (133 kts), the fighter has a 600-m (1,968-ft) landing run with brake parachute, increasing to 900 m (2,952 ft) on a wet runway. Similarly, the F-16A fighter has a 650-m (2,132-ft) landing run on a dry runway.

The F-16 features a small side-stick instead of a traditional control stick. This allows the pilot to fly the aircraft by moving his wrist only, increasing control precision. On the minus side, however, the pilot can use only his right hand to work the stick. The MiG-29 – both the production Fulcrum-A/B/C and the MiG-29M – have a conventional control column.

The F-16's ejection seat is inclined at a greater angle than the MiG-29's (30°). This allows the pilot to withstand higher G forces during vigorous maneuvering, but makes it harder to look back over

his shoulder. The F-16's one-piece frameless canopy offers better forward visibility.

Dimensionally, the two fighters are similar. The Fulcrum is slightly longer and has a bigger wingspan and wing area, but the F-16 is taller. The MiG-29's empty weight is higher, but normal TOW with six short-range AAMs is only 24-27% higher than the F-16's because of the lower fuel volume relative to total internal volume. In fact, the F-16's MTOW is higher than the MiG-29's.

The F-16 has a much bigger combat radius, but this is due mainly to the use of larger drop-tanks. The Fighting Falcon's ferry range is 3,900 km (2,166 nm) versus the MiG-29's 2,900 km (1,611 nm). On internal fuel only, however, the two fighters have almost identical range – 1,600 km (888 nm) for the F-16 and 1,500 km (833 nm) for the MiG-29.

In 1993 US analysts compared the F-16C and MiG-29 in typical combat configuration (i.e., with a 50% fuel load and two "dogfight AAMs" on the outer wing pylons). Their verdict was that the F-16 would have a minor advantage over the MiG during transonic maneuvering at low and medium altitude. According to US experts, in these conditions the MiG-29 would be handicapped by a G limit of 7 versus the F-16's 9 Gs, meaning the F-16 can make tighter turns.

The MiG-29's internal gun increases its dogfighting advantage. The IRST measures the target's coordinates and the laser rangefinder determines range. The asynchronous aiming method based on these data gives the Fulcrum excellent gunfire accuracy during maneuvering.

A "fly-off" between the F-16C and MiG-29 showed that the Fighting Falcon has a much higher roll rate thanks to its FBW control system and wing planform. Theoretically, this should give it a higher turn rate, reducing turn time. However, during the MiG-29's air show debut at Farnborough 1988, specialists noted that the Fulcrum could perform 360° turns without losing altitude – a crucial asset for a fighter. At 800 km/h (444 kts), turning radius is 350 m (1,148 ft); in the same situation the F-16 had a turning radius around 400 m (1,312 ft). At speeds above 400 km/h (222 kts), the MiG-29 can turn with a 225-m (738-ft) radius, pulling 3.8 Gs. At 10,000 m (32,808 ft) and Mach 0.9 the MiG-29 can pull 4.6-5.0 Gs in a turn.

Turn rate and linear acceleration are two of the most important factors determining a fighter's maneuverability. At Mach 0.85 the MiG-29's linear acceleration is 11 m/sec^2 (36 ft/sec^2) at S/L, which means the fighter can go from 500 km/h (277 kts) to 1,000 km/h (555 kts) in just 13 seconds. At 6,000 m (19,685 ft) and Mach 0.85, linear acceleration is 6.5 m/sec^2 (21.32 ft/sec^2).

Table 1.
Thrust-to-weight ratio

	Thrust-to-weight ratio:	
	combat*	takeoff
Mikoyan MiG-29SE/SM	1.52	1.08
Mikoyan MiG-29M	1.43	1.05
GD F-16C	1.05	1.09
McDD F/A-18C	1.00	0.93
Eurofighter EF2000	1.30	1.22
Dassault Mirage 2000-5	0.95	n/a

* At 1000 m (3,280 ft) and Mach 1.0 with a full internal fuel load

Coupled with excellent aerodynamics, the higher thrust-to-weight ratio gives the MiG-29 an advantage in maneuverability over its opponents.

The Fulcrum was a tough competitor for the GD F-16 on the world weapons market. Even though the avionics were considered rather primitive, the MiG-29 did exceptionally well in mock combat with Western fighters, both in Western and Eastern Europe. (Yefim Gordon)

The F-16C Fighting Falcon demonstrator, drawn from the 52 FW, is based at Spangdahlen AFB in western Germany at RIAT 2004, the giant Royal Air Force Benevolent Fund Airshow in the United Kingdom. (Yefim Gordon)

Table 2.
Rate of climb at 1,000 m (3,280 ft) and Mach 0.9 with a full internal fuel load

	Rate of climb, m/sec (ft/sec)
Mikoyan MiG-29SE	330 (1,082.67)
Mikoyan MiG-29M	320 (1,049.86)
GD F-16C	265-275 (869.42-902.23)
McDD F/A-18C	256 (839.89)
Eurofighter EF2000	300 (984.25)
Dassault Mirage 2000-5	285 (935.0)

Table 3.
Maximum turn rate at 3,000 m (9,842 ft) with 50% fuel

	Turn rate, deg/sec
Mikoyan MiG-29SE	23.5
Mikoyan MiG-29M	22.8
GD F-16C	21.5
McDD F/A-18C	20.0
Eurofighter EF2000	22.0
Dassault Mirage 2000-5	20.0

Table 4.
Specific wing loading at takeoff

	Wing loading, kg/m2 (lb/sq. ft)
Mikoyan MiG-29SE	403 (1,963)
Mikoyan MiG-29M	439 (2,139)
GD F-16C	435 (2,119)
McDD F/A-18C	420 (2,046)
Eurofighter EF2000	300 (1,461)

Table 5.
G limits of fourth-generation fighters

	Airframe G limit	Max G force in a turn
Mikoyan MiG-29SE	9.0	7.0
Mikoyan MiG-29M	9.0	7.0
GD F-16C	9.0	6.4
McDD F/A-18C	7.5	6.2
Eurofighter EF2000	9.0	7.0

Table 6.
Acceleration from 600 to 1,000 km/h (333-555 kts) at 1,000 m (3,280 ft)

	Acceleration time, sec
Mikoyan MiG-29SE	13.5
Mikoyan MiG-29M	13.5
GD F-16C	14.0
McDD F/A-18C	18.0
Eurofighter EF2000	14.0

The upgraded fire-control radars of the latest MiG-29 versions have a large field of view. In the MiG-29M's Phazotron N-010 "Zhuk" radar and the Phazotron N-019M "Topaz" of the MiG-29S, the beam is scanned in azimuth through 180° and 140°, respectively. By comparison, the Hughes Electronics AN/APG-65 radar fitted to the F/A-18C and the F-16C's Westinghouse AN/APG-68 have 140° and 120° scanning in azimuth, respectively.

Western and Russian assessments of the fighters' armament, WCSs, and combat potential differ. US specialists claim that the F-16A's Westinghouse AN/APG-66 radar is superior to the N-019, having, for example, 20% longer detection range. MAPO-MiG, however, maintains that the N-019 has longer range not only than the AN/APG-66 but the much more powerful AN/APG-65.

Table 7.
Fire Control radar performance data

	N-019	AN/APG-66	AN/APG-65
Weight, kg (lbs)	250 (551.14)	160 (352.73)	224 (493.82)
Volume, m3 (cu. ft)	n/a	0.11 (3.88)	0.12 (4.23)
Scanner diameter	n/a	0.6 m (1 ft 11.62 in.)	0.7 m (2 ft 3.55 in.)
Mean radiation power, W	n/a	150-250	400-450
Aerial target detection range, km (nm)*:			
in open airspace	75 (41)	40 (22)	65 (36)
in "look-down/shoot-down" mode, forward hemisphere	65 (36)	n/a	60 (33)
in "look-down/shoot-down" mode, rear hemisphere	35 (19)	n/a	40 (22)

* Fighter-type targets with an RCS of 3 m2 (32.25 sq. ft)

WARBIRDTECH
S E R I E S

Table 8.
Weapons control system data of fourth-generation fighters

	MiG-29SE	MiG-29M	F-16C	F/A-18C	EF2000
-Fire control radar					
Model	Phazotron N-019ME	Phazotron N-010	Westinghouse AN/APG-68	Hughes AN/APG-65	GEC-Marconi ECR90
Aerial target detection range, km (nm)*: in open airspace	60-70 (33-38)	80 (44)	50-60 (27-33)	60-65 (33-36)	70-80 (38-44)
in "look-down/shoot-down" mode, forward hemisphere	60 (33)	80 (44)	50-60 (27-33)	60 (33)	70 (38)
in "look-down/shoot-down" mode, rear hemisphere	30-35 (16-19)	40-50 (22-27)	30-35 (16-19)	35-40 (19-22)	40 (22)
Targets tracked	10	10	10	10	10
Targets attacked simultaneously	2	4	4	4	4
Scanning in azimuth	140°	180°	120°	120°	140°
Surface ship detection range, km (nm)**	n/a	120-150 (66-83)	120-150 (66-83)	120-150 (66-83)	120-150(66-83)†
Optoelectronic targeting system					
Aerial target detection range, km (nm)*: Head-on mode	n/a	10 (5.5)	none	none	n/a
pursuit mode	15 (2.7)	30 (16)	none	none	n/a
Laser rangefinder	yes	yes	yes‡	yes‡	No
Use in strike mode	no	yes	yes‡	yes‡	yes†
Active ECM	yes	yes	yes	yes	Yes

** Surface ship with an RCS of 3,000 m2 (32,258 sq. ft)   † To be introduced around 2005   ‡ Podded laser ranger/designator only

Table 9.
Maximum air-to-air missile launch range of fourth-generation fighters

	Medium-range AAMs in head-on mode	Medium-range AAMs in pursuit mode	Short-range AAMs in pursuit mode
MiG-29M	60 km (33 nm)	27 km (15 nm)	20 km (11 nm)
MiG-29	50 km (27 nm)	20 km (11 nm)	20 km (11 nm)
F-16C	40-45 km (22-25 nm)	18-20 km (10-11 nm)	18-20 km (10-11 nm)
F/A-18C	40-45 km (22-25 nm)	18-20 km (10-11 nm)	18-20 km (10-11 nm)

Table 10 at right illustrates the so-called combined combat efficiency quotient calculated by MAPO-MiG experts. This is a relative unit that includes the performance of the WCS and other mission avionics, the fighter's top speed in intercept mode, and weapons characteristics.

In dogfight mode the MiG-29's combined combat efficiency quotient, which here includes the characteristics of the ESM suite and the aircraft's acceleration as well, is even higher (see below).

Table 10.
Combined combat efficiency quotient of fourth-generation fighters in intercept mode

Mikoyan MiG-29SE	0.82
Mikoyan MiG-29SM	0.82
Mikoyan MiG-29M	1.00
GD F-16C	0.76
McDD F/A-18C	0.85
Dassault Mirage 2000-5	0.68
Eurofighter EF2000	0.9-1.0

Table 11.
Combined combat efficiency quotient of fourth-generation fighters in dogfight mode

Mikoyan MiG-29SE	0.90
Mikoyan MiG-29SM	0.90
Mikoyan MiG-29M	1.00
GD F-16C	0.79
McDD F/A-18C	0.65
Dassault Mirage 2000-5	0.82
Eurofighter EF2000	0.9-1.0

In strike mode, the F-16 is superior to the MiG-29 due to its higher MTOW. For example, with 2,000 kg (4,409 lbs) of bombs and two R-60M AAMs, the MiG-29 can only carry a single drop-tank. With a similar ordnance load, the F-16 can carry three drop-tanks, giving it longer range. Besides, the Fighting Falcon has aerial refueling capability which early production versions of the Fulcrum lack (introduced under a mid-life update program only). According to US experts, with two 900-kg (1,984-lb) bombs and two AIM-9 Sidewinder short-range AAMs, the F-16C has a 1,200-km (666-nm) combat radius on a "hi-lo-hi" mission profile; in similar conditions (two 900-kg bombs, two R-60M "dogfight AAMs", "hi-lo-hi") the MiG-29's combat radius is 500 km (277 nm). With the same armament on a "lo-lo-lo" mission profile, the two fighters' combat radius should be 740 km (411 nm) and 315 km (175 nm), respectively.

Table 12.
Combined combat efficiency quotient of fourth-generation fighters in strike mode

Mikoyan MiG-29SE	0.34
Mikoyan MiG-29SM	0.75
Mikoyan MiG-29M	1.00
GD F-16C	1.00
McDD F/A-18C	1.00
Dassault Mirage 2000-5	0.70
Eurofighter EF2000	0.8-1.0

According to Russian analysts, combat radius in supersonic (Mach 1.5) intercept mode with four medium-range AAMs, two short-range AAMs, and three drop-tanks is 410 km (227 nm) for the MiG-29M, 389 km (216 nm) for the F-16C, 370 km (205 nm) for the F/A-18C, and 345 km (191 nm) for the MiG-29S. In low-level penetration mode (200

m/656 ft) with drop-tanks, the fighters have a combat radius of 385 km (213 nm), 400 km (222 nm), 372 km (206 nm), and 340 km (188 nm), respectively. Thus, Russian and US fourth-generation light fighters are similar in range.

Table 13.
Summarized combat efficiency evaluation of fourth-generation fighters

	Combined combat efficiency quotient	
	air-to-air mode	strike mode
Mikoyan MiG-29SE	0.86	0.34
Mikoyan MiG-29SM	0.86	0.75
Mikoyan MiG-29M	1.00	1.00
GD F-16C	0.78	1.00
McDD F/A-18C	0.79	1.00
Dassault Mirage 2000-5	0.75	0.70
Eurofighter EF2000	0.9-1.0	0.8-1.0

Table 14.
Cost-effectiveness of fourth-generation fighters

	Mikoyan MiG-29SM	Mikoyan MiG-29SE	GD F-16C	McDD F/A-18C	Dassault Mirage 2000-5
air-to-air mode	1.0	1.23	0.87	0.75	0.76
strike mode	1.0	0.74	1.02	0.88	0.67

Table 15.
Reliability and serviceability parameters of fourth-generation fighters

	Mikoyan MiG-29SE	Mikoyan MiG-29M	GD F-16C	McDD F/A-18C
Operational readiness quotient	0.9	0.9	0.8	0.85
Specific maintenance labor intensity, man-hours per flight hour	11.3	11.0	18	16-18
MTBF, hrs	13.6	7.3	2.9	3.7
Airframe life, hrs	7,000	7,000	8,000	8,000
Relative cost	0.7	0.8	0.7	1.0

The above data indicates the F-16 is an air superiority fighter, optimized for air-to-air combat at subsonic and transonic speeds at low and medium altitude. The F-16's high MTOW also gives it strike capability. While the MiG-29 was conceived as an air superiority fighter, its early versions had limited strike capability; however, it is effective in the air defense role against high-flying high-speed targets.

MAPO-MiG calculations show that the MiG-29SE and MiG-29SM are a much more cost-effective solution as compared to their Western counterparts, as illustrated by Table 15 below.

MAPO-MiG also believes that the latest versions of the MiG-29 have better reliability and serviceability than the US competitors. MTBF is 7.3 hrs for the MiG-29M and 13.6 hrs for the MiG-29S versus 3.7 hrs for the F/A-18C and 2.9 hrs for the F-16C. Specific maintenance labor intensity is 11 man-hours per flight hour for the MiG-29M/S,

compared to 16 hrs for the F/A-18C and 18 hrs the F-16C during the initial service (IOC) period.

Of course, any analysis should be taken with a grain of salt. Analysts are never completely objective on either side, and of course all companies try to advertise their aircraft. Still, the MiG-29's impressive displays at various air shows speak for themselves.

Also, appraisals by Western experts – and not least fighter pilots – show beyond doubt that the Fulcrum is, and ought to be, treated with respect.

Table 16.
Comparative performance data of MiG-29 and the best Western fighters

	MiG-29SE	MiG-29M	F-16C	F/A-18C	EF2000
Powerplant	2xIzotov RD-33	2xIzotov RD-33K	Pratt&Whitney Electric F100-PW-220	2xGeneral F404-GE-400	2xEurojet EJ2000
Rating in full afterburner, kgp (lb st)	2x8,300 (2x18,386)	2x8,800 (2x19,400)	12,300 (27,116)	2x7,300 (2x16,093)	2x9,175 (2x20,227)
Normal TOW, kg (lbs)	15,300 (33,730)	16,680 (36,772)	12,100 (26,455)	15,700 (34,611)	15,000 (33,068)
MTOW, kg (lbs)	19,700 (43,430)	22,000 (48,500)	19,187 (42,300)	23,500 (51,807)	21,000 (46,296)
Internal fuel, kg (lbs)	3,832 (8,448)	4,460 (9,832)	3,104 (6,846)	4,900 (10,802)	4,000 (8,818)
External fuel, kg (lbs)	3,040 (6,702)	3,290 (7,253)	3,066 (6,760)	3,100 (6,834)	3,600 (7,936)
Ordnance load, kg (lbs)	4,000 (8,818)	4,500 (9,920)	5,443 (12,000)	4,500 (9,920)	6,500 (14,330)
Top speed, km/h (kts): at S/L	1,480 (822)	1,500 (833)	1,450 (805)	1,300 (722)	n/a
at altitude	2,450 (1,361)	2,500 (1,388)	2,000 (1,111)	1,900 (1,055)	2,200-2,300 (1,222-1,277)
Range, km (nm): on internal fuel only (at altitude)	n/a	2,000 (1,111)	1,600 (888)	2,200 (1,222)	1,800-2,200 (1,000-1,222)
with 3 drop-tanks	n/a	3,200 (1,777)	3,900 (2,166)	3,200 (1,777)	3,000-4,000 (1,666-2,222)

THE MiG-29 IN DETAIL

The MiG-29 is a twin-engine jet fighter of blended wing/body design. The fuselage (lifting body) and wings generate 40% and 60% of the total lift, respectively. At AOAs above 17° the proportion of the lift generated by the fuselage and leading-edge root extensions is increased. The airframe uses large extruded panels that reduce the number of stressed joints. Aluminum alloys (aluminum-lithium on the MiG-29K and MiG-29M) and high-strength steel are the main structural materials. Some airframe components subjected to high stress and/or temperature (e.g., the wing spars and aft fuselage structure) are made of titanium. Composites account for approximately 7% of airframe weight.

The airframe incorporates numerous access panels for ease of maintenance.

Fuselage (Lifting Body)

The fuselage is a semi-monocoque stressed-skin structure with 10 mainframes interspersed with regular frames and bulkheads. Structurally, the fuselage consists of three subassemblies: The forward fuselage (up to mainframe 4), center fuselage (mainframes 4 through 7), and rear fuselage (mainframes 7 through 10) incorporating the engine bays (mainframes 7 and 8) and aft bay.

The forward fuselage includes the ogival glass-fiber radome, the forward equipment bay, the pressurized cockpit, two avionics bays aft of the cockpit, and the nosewheel. The radome mounts the PVD-18 main pitot boom with horizontal vortex generators, the radar scanner, and the marker beacon receiver antenna.

The forward equipment bay houses the radar set and IRST/laser ranger; the transparent sensor "ball" of the latter is mounted dorsally, offset to starboard. The undersurface of the bay mounts IFF transponder, ATC, SHORAN and radio altimeter antennas, and the air data system's yaw vane; AOA vanes are mounted on both sides. A PVD-7 backup pitot is mounted on the starboard side of the bay (the MiG-29K and MiG-29M have a third pitot head mounted ventrally beneath the cockpit). The IFF interrogator antenna is mounted ventrally or dorsally (ahead of the windscreen), depending on the version. On the MiG-29K, the forward equipment bay also houses a retractable refueling probe offset to port.

The pilot sits on a Zvezda K-36DM zero-zero ejection seat set at a

The nose section of the MiG-29 houses the radar. (Yefim Gordon)

16° angle; the guide rails are attached to the aft cockpit bulkhead (frame No. 2). Seat height can be adjusted within ±85 mm (3.34 in.) to suit different pilots. Downward view over the nose is 14°.

The leading-edge root extensions (LERXes) built integrally with the fuselage begin at frame 1. Their area is 4.71 m² (50.64 sq. ft); leading-edge sweep is 73° 30'. The port LERX houses the internal gun and its ammo box (frames 1 through 3), while the starboard LERX accommodates air conditioning equipment. The port LERX features a gun blast panel made of heat-resistant steel near the gun muzzle and numerous cooling vents in the gun bay's upper skin between frames 2 and 3. Each LERX incorporates two dielectric panels over various aerials depending on the version (IFF, ATC, RHAWS, and/or ECM).

The main engine air intakes are mounted ventrally on the LERXes between frames 3 and 4. On the Fulcrum-A/B/C the LERXes have a rounded leading edge and incorporate auxiliary dorsal air intakes between frames 3-D and 4; the MiG-29K and MiG-29M have sharp-edged LERXes with no dorsal air intakes.

The MiG-29UB trainer differs markedly in forward fuselage design. Mainframe 1 is moved forward by 900 mm (2 ft 11.43 in.), increasing the pressurized cockpit's length to some 3 m (9 ft 10 in.). The trainee and instructor sit in tandem on identical K-36DM ejection seats enclosed by a common aft-hinged canopy; the latter incorporates a retractable periscope for the instructor, improving his forward view on takeoff and landing. All flight instruments and indicators are identical in both cockpits. The electric system's overload protection panel is moved forward from equipment bay No. 2 to a space between the front seat and rear instrument panel.

Since the MiG-29UB lacks radar, the nosecone is made almost entirely of metal, incorporating only a small dielectric fairing over the marker beacon receiver antenna. The forward equipment bay houses the IRST/LR, automatic control system components, and avionics. Thus Mikoyan managed to make the trainer completely identical with the Fulcrum-A

aft of mainframe 3 at the expense of only a 100-mm (3.93-in.) increase in overall length.

The centre fuselage of the MiG-29, MiG-29S/SD/SE/SM, and MiG-29UB incorporates three main integral fuel tanks and the main wheel wells. Tank No. 1 is limited by frames 4 and 5, tank No. 2 by frames 5 and 6, and tank No. 3 by frames 6 and 7.

With the radome removed, the nose of a MiG-29 shows the twist-cassegrain antenna of the N-019 Topaz radar. (Yefim Gordon)

The port RD-33 turbofan of Fulcrum-A with the large one-piece cowling removed for servicing, showing details of the engine. (Yefim Gordon)

Cockpit canopy of a Fulcrum-A. (Yefim Gordon)

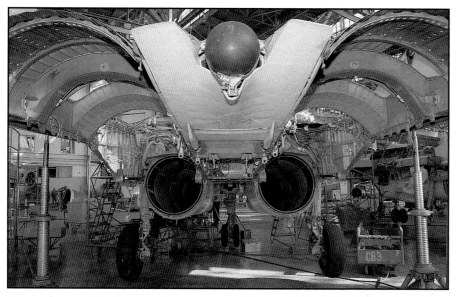

Engine bays and brake parachute container. This particular MiG-29 has the engines removed. (RSK MiG)

The last mentioned tank is the main structural element of the fuselage, absorbing the vertical loads from the wings, engines, and main gear units. Frame 6 incorporates the forward fitting of the centreline drop-tank and frame 7 features the engines' forward fittings. The main gear units are attached to special box structures fitting in between frames 6 and 7.

Frames 7 and 8 delimit the engine bays. Integral fuel tank No. 3-A split into two sections is located between frames 7 and 7-Zh. A bay in the aft fuselage houses the auxiliary power unit and the single accessory gearbox with associated generators, fuel, oil, and hydraulic pumps.

The aft fitting of the centerline drop-tank is located at frame 8. Further aft is the rear bay, mounting the tail unit and afterburners. Frame No. 9 incorporates attachment points for the airbrakes and brake parachute canister, as well as the engines' rear fittings. The airbrakes are hydraulically actuated. The brake parachute has an area of 17 m² (182.79 sq. ft).

The MiG-29K and MiG-29M have a different aft fuselage structure with a single large airbrake between frames 8 and 9 and a non-integral fuel tank (No. 3-B) added between frames 7 and 8. The MiG-29K is also equipped with an arrestor hook attached to frame 8.

Wings

Wings are a cantilever all-metal mid-wing monoplane of trapezoidal planform. They have a leading-edge sweep of 42°, anhedral 3°, taper 4.41, and aspect ratio of 3.5. The wings utilize TsAGI P-177 airfoil. Area of the wings proper (excluding LERXes) is 38.056 m² (409.2 sq. ft); chord is 5.6 m (18 ft 4.47 in.) at root and 1.27 m (4 ft 2.00 in.) at tip.

The wings have a three-spar structure with two false spars ahead of the wing torsion box and a third false spar aft of it, 16 ribs, and upper and lower skins reinforced by stringers. The outer wings are attached to the fuselage by five fittings each at frames 6, 6 V, and 7. The wing torsion box doubles as an integral fuel tank.

The wings have three-section leading-edge (LE) flaps, one-piece trailing-edge (TE) flaps, and ailerons. The LE flaps are deflected 20° by six hydraulic actuators each (one inboard, two on the central section, and three outboard). The TE flaps are deflected 25° for takeoff and landing by single hydraulic actuators equipped with uplocks; the high-lift devices move together. LE and TE flap area is 2.35 m² (25.26 sq. ft) and 2.84 m² (30.53 sq. ft), respectively. The ailerons have an area of 1.45 m² (15.59 sq. ft) and are deflected through +15°/-25° by RP-280A hydraulic actuators.

Each wing incorporates attachment points for three weapons pylons. The innermost pylons are attached to the spars in three places, the others in two. The wingtips mount navigation lights, RHAWS, and (on some versions) ECM antennas.

The MiG-29M features two-section leading-edge flaps. The MiG-29K has a radically different wing design; the wings are made of steel, not Al-Li alloy as on the M, and fold upwards for carrier stowage. Wingspan is increased by 630 mm (2 ft 0.8 in.) to 11.99 m (39 ft 4.04 in.), slightly increasing wing area; wings folded span is 7.8 m (25 ft 7.08 in.). Likewise, two-section leading-edge flaps are fitted, and the conventional ailerons are replaced by flaperons of slightly reduced area. The capacity of the wing tanks is identical to that of the Fulcrum-A/B/C. The MiG-29K and MiG-29M have two additional underwing hardpoints.

Nose gear unit. (Yefim Gordon)

Tail Unit

The slab stabilizers (stabilators) are mounted on the outer sides of the engine nacelles. They move symmetrically for roll control and differentially for pitch control. Leading-edge sweep is 50°, with anhedral at 3° 30'. The stabilators utilize TsAGI S-11S airfoil. Span is 7.78 m (25 ft 6.29 in.) and total area 7.05 m² (75.80 sq. ft); the MiG-29K and MiG-29M have increased-area stabilators with extended chord resulting in a characteristic "dogtooth."

Each stabilator is a single-spar structure with a false spar, 16 ribs, upper and lower skins, and a honeycomb core-composite trailing edge. RP-280A hydraulic actuators mounted on aft fuselage at frame 10 control the stabilators. The skewed axles are rigidly attached to the stabilators, turning in bearings mounted on frames 9 and 10. Stabilator deflection is +15°/-25° on takeoff and landing and +5° 45'/-17° 45' in cruise flight.

The twin fins with fillets and inset rudders are attached to the aft fuselage bay outboard of the engine nacelles.

The main gear units. (Yefim Gordon)

The fins are canted 6° outboard; leading-edge sweep is 47° 50′, total fin area 10.1 m² (108.6 sq. ft), and total rudder area 1.25 m² (13.44 sq. ft).

Each fin is a two-spar carbon fiber reinforced plastic (CFRP) structure with front and rear false spars, nine ribs, skins, and a honeycomb-core trailing edge. Structurally, the fins consist of rectangular root sections attached to the aft fuselage, detachable trapezoidal upper sections, and root fillets with 75° leading-edge sweep. Each rudder is mounted on three brackets and has a nose section and a honeycomb-core trailing edge. All aircraft manufactured from 1984 onwards have rudders with 21% longer chord extending beyond the fin trailing edge. The rudders are deflected ±25° by RP-270 hydraulic actuators mounted in the root sections. The fins have glass-fiber tips housing communications radio and ATC/SIF aerials (port fin) and IFF and GCI command link aerials (starboard fin).

Fulcrum-As built from 1984 onwards, Fulcrum-Cs, and the MiG-29S/SD/SE/SM have strake-like structures ahead of the fin fillets housing BVP-30-26 chaff/flare dispensers. These are absent on early-production Fulcrum-As, the MiG-29UB and MiG-29K, and MiG-29M prototypes. Early-production Fulcrum-As featured twin ventral fins outboard of the engine nacelles. These were deleted on later aircraft, as directional stability was found to be adequate without them.

Landing Gear

The MiG features hydraulically retractable tricycle landing gear; wheel track 3.09 m (10 ft 1.65 in.), wheelbase 3.645 m (11 ft 11.5 in.). All three units are equipped with oleo-pneumatic shock absorbers. The

The 1,500-lit. centerline drop-tank awaits installation. (Victor Drushlyakov)

nosewheels are fitted with a scraper-type mud/snow/slush guard for FOD protection.

The main units retract forward; the axes of the retraction hinges are

Three different views of the MiG-29 wing. (Yefim Gordon)

The wingtip of the Fulcrum shows the ECM antennas. (Yefim Gordon)

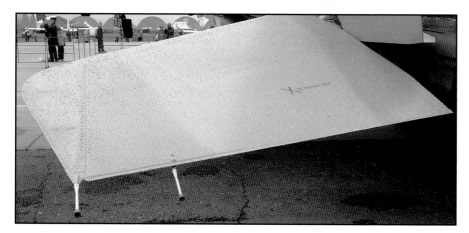

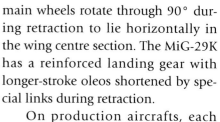

tilted outboard and aft so that the main wheels rotate through 90° during retraction to lie horizontally in the wing centre section. The MiG-29K has a reinforced landing gear with longer-stroke oleos shortened by special links during retraction.

On production aircrafts, each wheel well is closed by three doors, one of which is attached to the retraction jack. All doors remain open when the gear is down.

Powerplant

All versions except the MiG-29M and MiG-29K are powered by two Klimov NPP (Izotov) RD-33 afterburning turbofans rated at 5,040 kgp (11,111 lb st) at full military power, 5,600 kgp (12,345 lb st) at minimum afterburner, and 8,300 kgp (18,298 lb st) in full afterburner.

The RD-33 is a two-shaft turbofan with a bypass ratio (BPR) of 0.475, a four-stage axial low-pressure (LP) compressor, an adjustable nine-stage high-pressure (HP) compressor, an annular combustion chamber, a single-stage air-cooled HP turbine, a single-stage air-cooled LP turbine, an afterburner, and a convergent-divergent axisymmetric supersonic nozzle. Core and bypass flows are mixed aft of the turbine.

For greater reliability, the combustion chamber is equipped with an oxygen-feed system. It increases the

The Fulcrum's tailplane and pivot bearing. (Yefim Gordon)

chances of a successful relight at high altitudes with thin air. It also prevents flameouts caused by gas ingestion during gun firing and missile launches. The RD-33 is virtually immune to surge during violent maneuvers – even at negative airspeed during a tailslide.

Specific fuel consumption (SFC) is 2.05 kg/kgp·hr (lb/lb st·hr) in full afterburner and 0.77 kg/kgp·hr at full military power. The engine accelerates from idling RPM to full military power in three or four seconds, and another two seconds is needed to engage full afterburner. In case of

An un-mounted pair of under-wing ferry tanks. (Yefim Gordon)

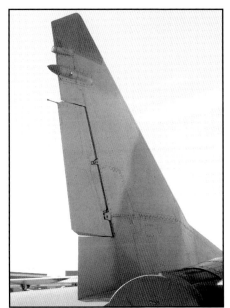

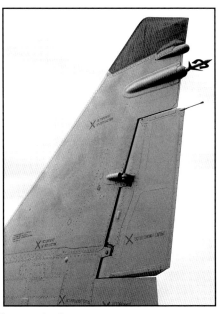

Five different views of the standard port and starboard on the tailfins of a MiG-29. (Yefim Gordon)

need, however, the RD-33 can go from idling RPM to full afterburner in just four seconds.

The engine is 4.26 m (13 ft 11.71 in.) long, with a maximum overall diameter of 1.0 m (3 ft 3.37 in.) and an inlet diameter of 0.75 m (2 ft 5.52 in.). Dry weight is 1,050 kg (2,314 lbs), which amounts to a weight/thrust ratio of 0.126. Engine life is 1,400 hrs (RD-33 Srs 2) or 2,000 hrs (RD-33 Srs 3); time between overhauls (TBO) is 700 and 1,400 hrs, respectively. The engines are controlled via mechanical linkages by throttles located on the port cockpit console.

The MiG-29K is powered by RD-33K engines uprated to 5,500 kgp (12,125 lb st) at full military power and 8,800 kgp (19,400 lb st) in full afterburner with a 9,400-kgp (20,723 lb st) contingency rating for high gross weight carrier takeoffs. A modified version of the RD-33K without this contingency rating powers the MiG-29M. The RD-33K is equipped with a FADEC system featuring the NR-59A fuel pump, RSF-59A regulator, and ESU-21 digital control unit. Afterburner SFC is improved to 1.97 kg/kgp hr and weight/thrust ratio to 0.119.

The engines are inclined 4° upwards and set at 1.5° "toe-in" in spaced nacelles. The adjustable supersonic air intakes are raked and have rectangular cross sections at the inlets changing to circular at the compressor faces. To prevent boundary layer ingestion, the intakes are set at a distance from the wing undersurface so that the upper intake lip acts as a boundary layer splitter plate. A vee-shaped fairing spilling the boundary layer connects the intake lip to the wing.

The horizontal airflow control ramps create four shock waves, optimizing the airflow for various flight modes (subsonic, transonic, and supersonic). These consist of four segments; the first (i.e., the splitter plate) is fixed at a 6° angle, the others are hydraulically actuated. The rearmost segment is perforated to spill the boundary layer via triple dorsal windows closed by metal mesh.

The MiG-29K, MiG-29M, and MiG-29SMT have redesigned air intakes with movable lower lips and no dorsal blow-in doors. FOD protection is offered by hinged grids that retract after takeoff to lie flat against the bottom of the inlet ducts, trap-

ping any foreign objects retained by them. The main wheel well walls are perforated to admit additional air at low speed. Besides all this, the MiG-29K and MiG-29M have reprofiled inlet ducts to cater for the higher mass flow of the uprated RD-33K engines.

On the ground the engines can be started singly or simultaneously by means of the NPP Klimov (Izotov) GTDE-117 auxiliary power unit (jet fuel starter) located in a bay in the aft fuselage between the engine nacelles. In flight, the engines can be restarted by windmilling at speeds as low as 300 km/h (166 kts).

The APU is fired up by an ST-115B starter-generator, using ground power or batteries. The APU provides electric and hydraulic power when the engines are shut down, allowing the aircraft's systems to be checked without using ground power – an undoubted asset on tactical airstrips where support equipment may be unavailable.

Separating engine accessories from the engines minimizes disconnecting operations during an engine change. The engines are extracted downwards and enclosed by one-

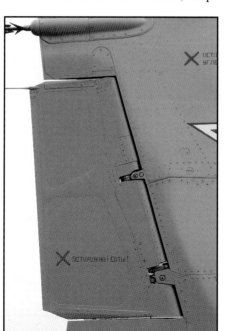
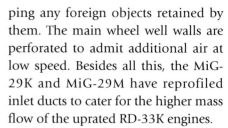
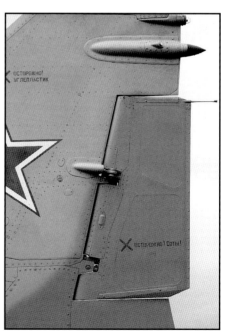

The Fulcrum rudders. (Yefim Gordon)

piece cowlings with quick-release fasteners; this means that a team of four technicians can change an engine in just 2 hrs 15 min.

Fuel System

Apart from its obvious purpose, the fuel system maintains the aircraft's CG, cools engine oil and bleeds air for the air conditioning system (on the MiG-29S/SE only) and the radar set (in the latter case by means of a fuel/glycol heat exchanger). Fuel system components and hydraulic tanks are located inside the fuel tanks for better survivability.

On the Fulcrum-A (including the MiG-29SD) and MiG-29UB, internal fuel is carried in four fuselage integral tanks and two wing tanks. Total internal fuel capacity is 4,300 lit. (946 Imp. gal.), amounting to 3,200 kg (7,054 lbs) of usable fuel at a specific fuel gravity of 0.785 g/cm.

On the Fulcrum-C, the capacity of fuselage tank No. 1 increases from 240 lit. (52.8 Imp. gal.) to 890 lit. (195.8 Imp. gal.), resulting in a characteristically bulged fuselage spine. This brings the total internal fuel capacity to 4,540 lit. (998.8 Imp. gal.) or 3,400 kg (7,495 lbs) of usable fuel.

Structural changes have increased internal fuel capacity to 5,810 lit. (1,278.2 Imp. gal.) for the MiG-29M, and 5,670 lit. (1,247.4 Imp. gal.) for the MiG-29K. The MiG-29K and MiG-29M have an internal fuel capacity of 5,720 lit. (1,258.4 Imp. gal.) or 4,460 kg (9,832 lbs) of usable fuel. The MiG-29K and MiG-29M also have provisions for three drop-tanks. The MiG-29SMT has an internal fuel capacity of approximately 5,300 lit. (1,166 Imp. gal.). To maintain CG position, the tanks are emptied in a certain sequence.

Armament

The MiG-29's weapons range allows it to fill the counter-air and strike roles, comprising an internal gun, short- and medium-range AAMs, unguided rockets, and free-fall bombs The MiG 29K, MiG-29M, and MiG-29SM/SMT can also carry guided air-to-surface missiles and guided bombs. Guided and unguided weapons are carried on four (MiG-29UB), six (Fulcrum-A/C), or eight (MiG-29K and MiG-29M) underwing hardpoints equipped with launch rails and/or ejector racks.

The MiG-29 communications, command link and IFF equipment aerials. (Yefim Gordon)

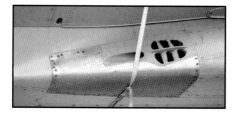

Cannon mount bay ventilation holes. (Yefim Gordon)

The TKB-687 (9A4071K) internal gun installation is housed in the port LERX and consists of a Gryazev/Shipoonov GSh-301 single-barrel 30-mm (1.18 caliber) automatic gun and associated ammunition box for 150 AO-18 rounds. Ammo capacity is reduced to 100 rounds on the MiG-29K and MiG-29M. Rate of fire is 1,500-1,800 rounds per minute, muzzle velocity 860 m/sec (2,821.5 ft/sec), and recoil force 6,000-7,500 kg (13,227-16,534 lbs).

A trigger on the stick electrically controls firing. The gun can fire continuously; expending the entire ammo supply in a single six-second burst, or in short bursts. Alternative firing modes are "automatic fire" (three-quarters of the ammo supply), "automatic fire with cutoff" (firing 25 rounds in a one-second burst each time the trigger is squeezed), and "training mode" (a 7-round burst each time the trigger is squeezed).

The GSh-301 is water-cooled, with additional air-cooling through vents in the gun bay to extend its service life. The gun can tolerate 2,000 shots; it is 1,978 mm (6 ft 5.87 in.) long and weighs 45 kg (99.2 lbs).

The MiG-29 (9.12 and 9.13) is armed with two Vympel R-27R medi-um-range AAMs and/or two, four, or six Vympel R-73 or Molniya R-60M short-range AAMs.

The R-27R (470) can destroy all manner of aerial targets, including RPVs and cruise missiles, in all weather conditions, day or night, over land and sea, even if the target maneuvers violently, returns fire, uses ECM, and/or generally misbehaves. Target flight level is 20-27,000 m (65-88,582 ft) and maximum target speed is 3,500 km/h (1,944 kts). The missile can be launched when the aircraft is pulling up to 5 Gs and the target is up to 10,000 m (32,808 ft) higher or lower.

The air-to-air weapons range of the MiG-29S/SD/SE/SM/SMT includes two R-27R/T/RE/TE medium-range AAMs (R 27R1/T1/RE1/TE1 for export), two, four, or six R-77 (RVV-AE) medium-range AAMs, and a like number of R-73 (R-73E) short-range AAMs. The R-77 is designed to destroy enemy fighters, bombers, attack and transport aircraft, and helicopters in all weather conditions, over land and sea, day or night, and in an ECM environment.

The MiG-29K and MiG-29M can carry two R-27RE/TE AAMs, two or four R-27R/T AAMs, two, four, six, or eight R-77s, and/or a like number of R-73s.

In the attack role, all versions of the MiG-29 can carry a range of unguided rockets, including two or four B-8M1 rocket pods with twenty 80-mm (3.15-in.) S-8 folding-fin aircraft rockets (FFARs) each and two or four 240-mm (9.44-in.) S-24B heavy unguided rockets on APU-68-85 launchers.

Avionics and Equipment

Weapons Control System

The MiG-29's WCS comprises of a fire-control radar for medium-range targeting and a short-range

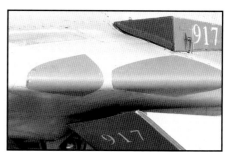

The aerial position in the wing LERX. (Yefim Gordon)

The MiG-29 wing LERX. (Yefim Gordon)

optoelectronic targeting system. It enables the aircraft to complete its mission (long-range intercept, dogfight, or strike) in all weather conditions, day or night, and in an ECM environment, operating singly or in a group.

The RLPK-29 complex can track up to ten targets at a time, automatically selecting a priority threat. The pilot can also manually designate a priority target. The radar determines the exact coordinates of the priority target as it is tracked. On the MiG-29SD/SE the system can engage two priority threats at a time and has a training mode simulating the target's evasive maneuvers and countermeasures. The system has an automatic self-test feature.

On the MiG-29SD/SE, the complex has a training mode simulating the target's evasive maneuvers and countermeasures and displays WCS test results.

The OEPrNK-29 consists of an OEPS-29 optoelectronic targeting system, an SN-29 navigation system, a Ts100 series digital processor, an

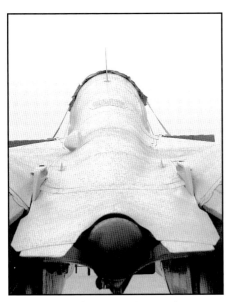

A rear view of the dorsal spine fairing and fuselage rear section of a MiG-29. (Yefim Gordon)

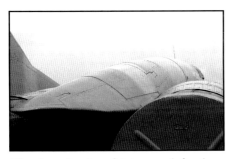

The dorsal spine fairing and fuselage rear section of a MiG-29SMT second prototype. (Yefim Gordon)

SUO-29M weapons selection system, an SEI-31 joint indication system (JIS) featuring the ILS-31 HUD, an FKP-EU gun camera, and multi-function control panels.

The OEPS-29 targeting system includes the KOLS (*izdeliye* 13S) infrared search & track/laser ranger designed by NPO "Gheofizika" and the "Schchel'-3UM" HMS ("Schchel'-3UM-1" for export). The IRST/LR, which can acquire targets independently or with data input from the radar, can determine the target's coordinates and range with greater accuracy than the radar. Since the IRST/LR does not emit electromagnetic pulse, it enables the fighter to attack covertly without switching on

the radar. Some performance figures are given below.

Detection range (fighter-type target):
   15 km (8.3 nm)
Steady tracking range:
   12 km (6.6 nm)
Laser ranger operating range:
   200-6,500 m (656-21,325 ft)
Large field of view:
   ±30° in azimuth, ±15° in elevation
Small field of view:
   ±15° in azimuth, ±15° in elevation
Scanning time:
   large field of view . . . . 3.5 sec
   small field of view . . . . 2.0 sec

The MiG-29M and MiG-29K are equipped with an OLS-M IRST/LR featuring a more sensitive IR sensor with cooling, a more powerful laser ranger, and a TV channel for long-range target identification. The IRST's detection range is 35 km (19.4 nm) in pursuit mode and 10 km (5.5 nm) in head-on mode. The TV channel's detection range and identification range are 10 km and 6 km (3.3 nm) respectively; the LR's maximum range is 8 km (4.4 nm).

The "Schchel'-3UM" HMS with NVU-2M goggles increases targeting efficiency in a dogfight, offering the "point and shoot" targeting mode. By turning his head towards the target the pilot supplies targeting data both to the IRST/LR and to the R-73 IR-homing AAMs. If the latter gets a lock-on, the pilot can fire missiles without waiting for target data from other systems to become available.

The MiG-29M has an upgraded navigation suite featuring an INS-84 inertial navigation system, an SVS-2Ts-U air data system, an A-331 SHORAN/ILS with a "Potok" (Stream) antenna and feeder system, an "Uragan" long-range radio navigation (LORAN) system, and a Ts080 digital processor. The MiG-29M has a slightly different SN-K "Oozel" (Knot) navigation suite featuring a "Resistor-K-42" SHORAN/ILS optimized for carrier operations instead of the A-331.

The attack results are documented by the FKP-EU gun camera that can photograph targets within 3,000 m (1.6 nm). The gun camera "fires" through the HUD glass and uses 35-mm film up to 30 m (98 ft) long; maximum camera speed is 10 frames per second.

These photos illustrate a MiG-29K Fulcrum D airbrake. (Yefim Gordon)

The main air intakes. This MiG-29 has the engine covers on. (Yefim Gordon)

The MiG-29M and MiG-29K tail cone. (Yefim Gordon)

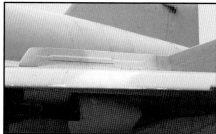

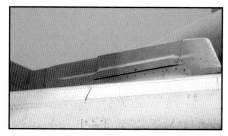

The MiG-29 fin root extensions with chaff/flare launchers. (Yefim Gordon)

Radio Navigation Equipment

The MiG-29's radio navigation suite comprises the ARK-19 ADF, the A-037 radio altimeter, the A-611 (RPM-76) marker beacon receiver, and the SO-69 ATC transponder. The ADF consists of a receiver, a control panel, and two aerials on the fuselage spine (an omni-directional blade aerial and a directional loop aerial). It enables navigation by means of ground VHF omni-directional range (VOR) beacons by determining the angle between the aircraft's longitudinal axis and the beacon's bearing. The ADF's range depends on the aircraft's flight level and the power of the VOR (e.g., a 500-watt beacon can be detected at 200-300 km/111-166 nm). The error margin is 3-5°.

The A-037 Doppler altimeter doubles as a ground proximity warning system (GPWS) when the gear and flaps are up. It consists of a transceiver, two aerials under the fuselage nose, and an electromechanical indicator. Measurement range is 0-1,000 m (3,280 ft). Early-production aircraft were equipped with the RV-15 (A-031)

altimeter; the MiG-29M and MiG-29K have the RV-21 (A-035) "Impul's" altimeter.

The A-611 receiver informs the pilot that he has passed the outer and inner marker beacons during his landing approach. A beep sounds in the pilot's headset when the aircraft passes the beacons. The SO-69 transponder transmits the aircraft's call sign, TAS, and altitude. These are displayed beside the aircraft's "blip" on the air traffic control (ATC) radar screen, allowing better air traffic control and flight safety, especially in an ECM environment in combat. ATC transponder aerials are located under the nose, in the port LERX and on both fins. The MiG-29M and MiG-29K are equipped with an improved SO-72 (A-511) ATC transponder.

Communications Equipment

The suite comprises an R-862 "Zhooravl'-30" (Crane) UHF radio, an SPU-9 intercom, and an R-855UM "Komar-2M" emergency radio. The R-862 radio is used for communication with other aircraft and ground control.

The SPU-9 intercom enables the pilot to use the radio and listen to VOR identification signals, warning and caution messages given by the "Almaz-UP" (Diamond) voice information module, and informing and warning "beeps" from various systems. On the ground it can be used for communication with ground crews who plug into a connector on the forward fuselage. Finally, on the MiG-29UB, the intercom can be used for communication between trainee and instructor.

IFF Equipment

The IFF system identifies aerial targets detected by the fire-control radar as "friendly," "identity unknown," or "hostile" and responds to "identify yourself" queries from other aircraft.

The interrogator aerial is located dorsally or ventrally ahead of the cockpit. Transponder aerials are located under the nose, in the LERXes, on the port fin, and (SRO-2 only) on the wingtips.

Electronic Support Measures Suite

The ESM suite warns the pilot that he is under attack, indicates possible directions from which he could be attacked, and diverts enemy missiles from the aircraft. The core of the MiG-29's ESM suite is the SPO-15LM (L006LM) "Beryoza" radar homing and warning system (RHAWS). With a warning "beep," the system informs the pilot that he is being "painted" by enemy radars. The joint indication system display then shows the direction and type of the radar and the signal's intensity.

The RD-33 engine jet nozzle and after-burner. (Yefim Gordon)

To disrupt the operation of land-based and shipboard air defense radars and sidetrack radar-homing AAMs and SAMs, the Fulcrum-C, MiG-29M, and MiG-29K are equipped with a "Gardeniya-1FU" (L203B) active jammer. The export version, "Gardeniya-1FUE" (L203BE), is fitted to the MiG-29SE. On the Fulcrum-C, the jammer works with the "Beryoza" RHAWS, using an L138 commutation module.

Depending on the type of enemy radar illuminating the aircraft, the jammer can emit high-frequency noise, low-frequency Doppler noise, or flashing interference signals. This allows it to neutralize at least two radars operating in continuous, quasi-continuous, or pulse-Doppler emission mode. The jammer covers a sector of the aircraft's rear hemisphere measuring ±60° in azimuth and ±30° in elevation.

The Fulcrum-A/C is equipped with two BVP-30-26M chaff/flare dispensers located on the wing upper surface ahead of the fin fillets and canted towards the aircraft's centerline. These are loaded with sixty 26-mm (1.02-in.) PPI-26 IRCM flares for protection against IR-homing missiles or PPR-26

chaff bundles for passive radar jamming, though the latter are seldom used. These are fired by the SUVP-29 control unit, which determines the firing sequence and duration.

On the MiG-29M and MiG-29K, the chaff/flare capacity is doubled, with two BVP-60-26 dispensers buried in the aft fuselage upper surface.

Command Link Equipment

The E502-20 "Biryuza" command-link system receives guidance signals, target coordinates, and tactical and interaction data from ground command (GCI) centers. The commands prepared by the CGI computer are transmitted as modulated HF signals and received by the "Bekas-R," then converted into standard digital or analog form and fed to the radar, automatic control system, JIS, intercom, etc. The main parameters transmitted via the command link system are the target's altitude and speed, range to target, closing speed, and required heading and elevation.

By customer request all export versions of the Fulcrum may be fitted with flight instruments marked in the Imperial system of measurement units, Western TACAN tactical radio navigation, IFF and VOR/ILS equipment, an SO-69M ATC transponder using internationally accepted frequencies (or a Cossor IFF transponder), GPS, and an extra Western communications radio.

Built-in Test Equipment/Crew Alerting System (BITE/CAS) and Data Recording Equipment

The MiG-29 features an "Ekran-03M" common test and crew alerting system. The "Ekran" BITE/CAS is built around a programmable data collection and processing module which diagnoses systems down to subsystem level, informs the pilot of critical systems failures, and records

these for ground personnel to deal with later. It enables an automated pre-flight systems check and monitors the aircraft's systems in flight. Malfunctions are memorized in priority order and automatically recorded on tape 20 seconds after touchdown along with the time of failure. 64 malfunction messages can be memorized and recorded and 256 alpha-numeric messages displayed in priority order.

The BITE/CAS and self-test modules of certain systems monitor more than 80% of the aircraft's systems and equipment. The VSS-1-4K light indication system informs the pilot of systems operating modes and malfunctions by means of green information lights, yellow caution lights, and red warning lights.

The "Almaz-UP" (P-591B) voice information module plays back 47 pre-recorded caution and warning messages, informing the pilot of dangerous flight modes and malfunctions. The most critical warning messages are also transmitted to the ATC operator by radio. The messages are triggered by sensors in the engines, intake ramp control, hydraulic, electric, life support and air data systems, and by the BITE/CAS.

The "Tester-UZLK" FDR tapes coded information about flight modes and systems operation to be used in normal mission evaluation or accident investigation. It is housed in a crashworthy capsule in the aft fuselage, and is switched on manually or automatically at the moment of unstick. The FDR records the engines' operating mode, RPM and exhaust gas temperature, fuel flow, intake ramp and landing gear position, G loads and pitch/roll/yaw rates, heading and vertical speed, operation of the WCS, automatic flight control, hydraulic, fire suppression and crew escape systems, marker beacon receiver, and comms radio.

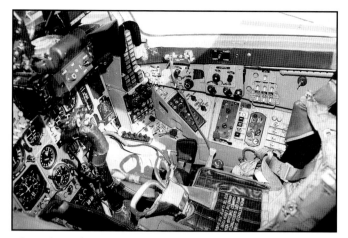

The Fulcrum's instrument panel and cockpit controls. (Yefim Gordon)

This is the MiG-29SMT-I instrument panel. (Yefim Gordon)

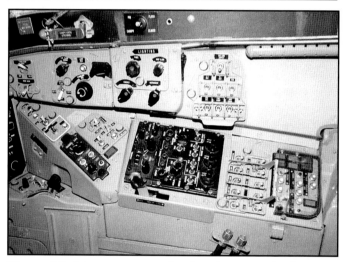

The modified instrument panel and cockpit controls of a modified German MiG-29. (via Thomas Muller)

This is a modified instrument panel of the MiG-29SMT-II. (Yefim Gordon)

This is the most modern MiG-29M2 instrument panel. (Yefim Gordon)

THE FUTURE

These two views are of a MiG-29OVT prototype, which was displayed on MAKS-2001 air show at Zhukovskiy. This version began trials in 2001 and features an MNPK digital fly-by-wire system. (Yefim Gordon)

The MiG-29 is currently in service with the air arms of more than 20 nations with future prospects of new exports and product improvement. For example, improved lateral stability and roll control introduced on the MiG-29S by optimising aileron and rudder movement, and modifying the automatic control system have increased the MiG-29SD/SE/SM's AOA limit to 28-30°, giving it better agility.

A further improvement in agility could be obtained by introducing thrust-vectoring control (TVC). The use of TVC both in the pitch and yaw channels offers sizeable advantages over pitch-only TVC while incurring only a negligible weight penalty.

To reduce pilot workload, the HOTAS principle is to be implemented. The traditional analogue flight instruments are replaced by an EFIS with multi-function color LCDs and conventional switches by a multi-function control panel. The cockpit also features an upgraded HUD. The finished result is similar to the definitive MiG-29M prototype.

Other possible improvements consist of the installation of an advanced ESM suite including an ELINT/SIGINT pack, an RHAWS, an infrared missile warning system, a

Two more views of the same aircraft repainted in 2003. Here it is displayed on MAKS-2003 air show and with the aerobatic team at the air show in August 2004 at Zhukovskiy. (Yefim Gordon)

The tail part of this MiG-29OVT prototype shows the thrust vectoring engines. These were Sarkisov RD-33-10M engines modified with KLIVT (Klimov Vectored Thrust) 360° thrust vectoring nozzles. (Yefim Gordon)

programmable active jammer, and chaff/flare dispensers. Additionally, the airframe is to be coated with RAMs to reduce radar signature.

Combat capability may be enhanced by installing a data link to GCI centres, AWACS aircraft, or other fighters. This enables the MiG-29 to operate jointly with other fighters (e.g., the Su-27 or MiG-31 Foxhound) and even SAM sites. In this case, MiG-31 and Su-30 two-seat interceptors can act as mini-AWACS aircraft, designating targets and guiding MiG-29s to them.

The WCSof the MiG-29SD/SE/SM is compatible with most Russian medium-range AAMs and IR-homing "dogfight AAMs" currently in production.

Operating costs are to be reduced by effective training of highly skilled maintenance personnel using the latest techniques and computerized teaching aids. For foreign operators, a joint aircraft maintenance center could be established.

MAPO specialists believe that this combined approach to improving the MiG-29 and stage-by-stage completion of the long-term upgrade program is ensuring that the Fulcrum remains in service well into the future. The resulting gap between third-generation fighters that are due to be phased out and fifth-generation fighters that are just entering flight test are bridged by today's fighters which are staying around for another 10 or 15 years – and the MiG-29 is one of the best among them.

Even now, many nations are showing an interest in the MiG-29SMT. Of course, the MiG-29SMT was developed primarily with the Russian Air Force in mind. Importantly, this is an affordable option for the long-suffering Russian defense budget. The Russian MoD plans to begin upgrading MiG-29s currently in service. Some 150 conversions are planned in all.

The MiG-29M2 prototype, also referred to as the MRCA, was displayed in August 2001 on MAKS-2001 air show at Zhukovskiy. This is a two-seat strike variant of the Fulcrum, and is optimized for low-level operations against high-value, high-risk targets. (Yefim Gordon)

MiG-29M2 cockpit and canopy. Improvements include folding wings and a Phazotron-NIIR Zhuk-M multimode radar. It made its maiden flight from Zhukovskiy on September 26, 2001. Note the neatly stowed refueling probe. (Yefim Gordon)

Two views of the MiG-29SMT-III (918 White) fighter prototype as displayed on MAKS-2001 air show at Zhukovskiy. The desert camouflage may indicate the intended future markets for this advanced version. (Yefim Gordon)

RSK MiG chief pilot Pavel Vlasov demonstrates the agility and sleek lines of the MiG-29M2. The aircraft is a land-based version of the naval MiG-29K. (Yefim Gordon)

MiG-29 Scale Model Kits

By Richard Marmo

When someone visits your model room, they're likely to find a very nice collection of modern fighter jets. An F-16, F-15, F-14, Tornado, and on and on. Even an Su-27. But wait a minute. Isn't something missing? What about the subject of this book – a MiG-29?

It can't be because models of the aircraft don't exist. They do, and some of them are very nice indeed. You can't say they don't make it in your scale, either, because MiG-29 kits are available in every standard scale from 1/32 to 1/144. There's also a healthy collection of aftermarket products for the superdetailer. In fact, just doing a search on Squadron.com will net you a grand total of 43 different items, including kits, decals, and a slew of Eduard photoetch detail parts. Believe me, if you haven't added a MiG-29 to your collection yet, you won't have any problem doing it. Let's look at some of the more readily available kits.

If you're looking for 1/32 scale, your only choice (unless Trumpeter announces one by the time this is published) is the Revell effort. Originally produced in 1991, it's really quite nice despite some contour/shape problems. Surface detail is both light and recessed. Included in the kit are a pair of turbofan engines intended to be installed in the model (where you can't see them), a basic radar behind a removable nose cone, centerline drop-tank, positionable canopy, and a full complement of Apex AA-10 and AA-11 missiles. Cockpit interior is typical for Revell in that time period, which means you will need to spend a little time there. Is it perfect? No (especially

Revell's 1/32-scale MiG-29 box. The finished model is 21-1/2 inches long, so the box is almost as big. It's substantial and is certainly an appropriate description.

if you're planning on entering it in a contest), but it builds into a very nice model – though not a truly accurate one – right out of the box, so think what you'd have if you put some effort into it. Besides, it's the only game in town (so far) if you love 1/32 scale. It is available at the present time from Revell of Germany. The price is $49.96, more or less, as this is written.

1/48-philes have at least four different kits to choose from, and three are produced by Academy. The odd kit out, which I found hiding under

The Revell kit box is big for a reason. It's crammed with parts.

my bench and had nearly forgotten it existed, was released by Monogram sometime between 1991 and 1993 as part of its Iron Curtain collection. With the fuselage split horizontally into two halves, raised surface detail and a weapons mix consisting of two AA-10 and four AA-8 missiles, it doesn't hold a candle to current kit standards.

However, if you're looking to add a 1/48-scale MiG-29 to your collection that's up to current standards, the Academy kits are the only way to

Here you see the nearly forgotten Monogram 1/48 version of the MiG-29.

go. Available three ways, you can have either a MiG-29A, MiG-29B, or MiG-29 Ukraine. The Ukraine version, in case you don't remember, was the aircraft flown by the Ukraine Flight Demonstration Team that wowed the crowd at the Farnborough Air Show in 1988.

Probably the best model of the MiG-29 yet in any scale is this Academy 1/48 scale MiG-29A and its two companion kits, the MiG-29B and MiG-29 Ukraine.

All three of these kits are essentially the same except for the markings and the fact that the MiG-29B is a two-seater. Quality is everything you'd want, including very light and delicate recessed surface detail, positionable canopy, positionable air brake, full weapons load of AA-10D, AA-11, and AA-8 missiles, and a beautifully done cockpit interior. Combine any of these kits with some of the photoetch detail sets and resin after-market components (such as ejection seats, exhaust nozzles, and wheel bays) and you'll have a real prize winner. Prices for these kits range from $26.00 to $27.00.

Devotees of 1/72 haven't been left out in the cold either. Italeri offers both a MiG-29A and a MiG-29UB. Typical of Italeri efforts, surface detail is delicately recessed with some of the parts being so small to the point that you need a pair of tweezers to handle them and an OptiVisor to find them. On the down side, cockpit interiors are relatively basic, so it's back to the after-market for detail sets and resin castings. All in all, these turn into very nice representations of the MiG-29 with just a little work. And at only $15.00 each.

Before anyone out there tells me that there have been other 1/72 kits of the MiG-29, I know there are. In fact, Squadron lists a MiG-29 from Hasegawa and a "Hi-Tech" MiG-29UB from Heller. Fujimi also produced one at one time, and who knows how many others are out there that are either no longer in production or have simply been supplanted by more recent and better efforts.

And finally, if you like your MiG-29 on the small side, take a look at a fourth (you heard me, fourth) Academy kit – this time in 1/144 scale. It used to be if you mentioned 1/144 scale, the only reaction you'd get was a sneer (at least where a single-seat fighter was concerned), which left you with the distinct impression that the very idea was beneath contempt. No more. 1/144 scale has gotten to be quite popular, so it's perfectly reasonable that a MiG-29 would appear in this size.

Despite being a mere 4 inches in overall length, the little puppy features recessed surface detail and a full load of missiles. You also get an actual cockpit, though it's limited to a basic tub and seat. I wonder who's going to be first to do a superdetailed interior? And you certainly can't beat the price at $4.75. By the way, that strange round object you see leaning up against the lower fuselage half is a good ol' American quarter (25-cent piece) to give you some idea of this kit's size.

With so many kits and scales to choose from, there's no reason not to add a MiG-29 to your collection. You can't even claim lack of reference material, because this book has everything you'll need on that score. Well, don't just sit there. Go buy a kit and start building!

Drop down to 1/72 and these two efforts from Italeri would likely be considered the best choices.

And in the miniscule 1/144 scale, it's Academy again. Note the quarter just to the left of the decal sheet to give some idea of the model's size.